THE
SEASONAL
KITCHEN

THE SEASONAL KITCHEN

EDITED BY

Laurie Ochoa

FOOD EDITOR

and the Food Staff of the Los Angeles Times,
Davilynn Furlow, *Deputy Food Editor*
Charles Perry, Russ Parsons, Barbara Hansen, *Staff Writers*
Donna Deane, *Times Test Kitchen Director*
Nick Cuccia, *News Editor* • Kathy Gosnell, *Copy Editor*
Anne Colby, *Book Project Copy Editor*
Tracy Crowe McGonigle, *Art Director*

Photography by Los Angeles Times Photo Staff

Los Angeles Times
A Times Mirror Company
Los Angeles, California

Los Angeles Times

Publisher: Mark H. Willes
Editor: Shelby Coffey III
Associate Editor and VP: Narda Zacchino

Los Angeles Times Syndicate
President & CEO: Jesse Levine
VP/GM Domestic: Steve Christensen

Director of Book Development: Don Michel

Food Editor: Laurie Ochoa
Book Designer: Tracy Crowe McGonigle

Library of Congress Catalogue Number (97-069892)
ISBN 1-883792-18-5
Copyright © 1997 Los Angeles Times

Published by the Los Angeles Times Syndicate
Times Mirror Square, Los Angeles, California 90053
A Times Mirror Company

First Printing October 1997

Printed in the USA

CONTENTS

spring
PAGE 16

summer
PAGE 44

fall
PAGE 80

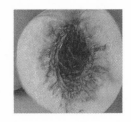

winter
PAGE 114

Introduction

There is a simple secret to becoming a great cook: fresh, seasonal ingredients. Neither years of cooking classes, nor thousands of dollars' worth of kitchen equipment will do you much good if you serve a cottony tomato in February. What does a tomato like that—out of season, out of flavor—really add to a meal? A slight amount of color? A bit of tomato texture? The cook must work hard to make that tomato even minimally palatable.

But a late-summer tomato, bursting with juice and flavor, is no work at all. With a handful of fresh basil, a tablespoon or two of olive oil and a sprinkling of coarse salt, that tomato, with maybe a hunk of rustic bread, can become a great meal.

Ingredients matter. Whether harvested from your own garden, bought directly from the growers at a farmers market or at a roadside stand or carefully selected from your neighborhood supermarket, locally grown seasonal produce is the cheapest and easiest way to make spectacular meals.

Much of what we do in the Los Angeles Times Food section is determined by the tempo of the seasons—spring's first flash of asparagus, winter's citrus explosion, fall's squash harvest and the days in mid-summer when it seems that the weight of sweet white peaches in the nation's produce sections threatens to alter the orbit of the earth.

We are lucky to live in Southern California, the heart of perhaps the world's greatest agricultural region, but great cooks make the most of the seasons no matter where they live. The spread of farmers markets throughout the nation and the growth of the organic farming industry are just two changes that have made it easier to eat the way we once did in this country—by the season.

For this book, we selected some of our favorite recipes from the pages of the Food section. They are recipes that show off the flavors of fruits and vegetables picked at the height of their season. But they are just a hint of what can be done with seasonal produce. Use this book for its recipes, but use it also for inspiration. Remember that the recipe for using a perfectly ripe peach is no recipe at all . . . just eat and enjoy.

—LAURIE OCHOA

A Guide to Seasonal Produce

Apples

Fall, Winter

September through November, sold from cold-storage year-round

•

Apricots

Late Spring, Summer

Begin in May, peak in mid-June, continue strong through July, slim supplies in August

Artichokes

Spring, Fall

At their best March through May, sold year-round, at their worst July through August, second season September through October

•

Asparagus

Spring

Traditional season March through June, strongest in April and May, sold year-round

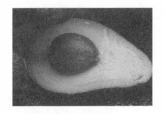

Avocados

Spring, Summer

At their best March through June, peak in May, Hass variety strong April to November, sold year-round

•

Bananas

Year-Round

Year-round, peak May through June

Basil

Summer

Best June through September, sold year-round

•

Beets

Year-Round

Strong April to October, best June through August

Belgian Endive

Spring

Year-round, begins strong in November, best March to June

•

Bell Peppers

Summer, Fall

Year-round, peak July through October

Blackberries

Summer

May through September, peak June through July

•

Blood Oranges

Winter, Spring

December through April

•

Blueberries

Summer

April to October, strong June through September, peak July and August

Boysenberries

Summer, Fall
August through January,
peak late summer through
early fall

Broccoli

Year-Round
Peaks in March

•

Broccoli Rabe

Year-Round
Strongest August through
March, weakest June
and July

•

Brussels Sprouts

Fall, Winter, Spring
Strongest October
through April

•

Cabbages

Year-Round

•

Cantaloupes

Summer
May through December,
best June to September
(related melons peak
August and September)

Cardoons

Fall, Winter
September to March

Carrots

Year-Round
Young carrots widely
available in February and
March

Cauliflower

Year-Round
Best September through
November

•

Celery

Year-Round
Peaks November and
December

•

Celery Root

Fall, Winter, Spring
Strong November through
April, best in November

•

Chanterelle Mushrooms

Winter, Spring
September through April,
strongest late spring

Cherries

Summer
May through August

•

Chicory

Year-Round

•

Chile Peppers

Year-Round
Some varieties more
abundant August to
November

•

Chinese Mustard Greens (Goi Choy)

Year-Round

•

Coconuts

Year-Round
Strongest October to
January

•

Collard Greens

Year-Round
Plentiful October to
May, strongest December
through April

Corn

Summer
Best June through
September, sold year-round

•

Common Herbs

*(Chives, Cilantro, Dill,
Mint, Parsley, Rosemary,
Sage, Tarragon, Thyme)*
Year-Round

•

Common
Mushrooms

*(Button, Crimini, Enoki,
Oyster, Portobello,
Shiitake)*
Year-Round

•

Cranberries

Fall, Winter
September to January,
strongest October through
November

Cranberry Beans

Summer, Fall
August through October

•

Crenshaw Melons

**Summer, Fall, Early
Winter**
July through December

•

Cucumbers

Year-Round
Pickling varieties most
abundant July and August

•

Dandelion Greens

Spring, Summer, Fall
Year-round, strong March
to December, peak April
and May

Dates

Fall, Winter
Peak October through
December, sold year-round

Eggplants

Year-Round
Strongest July and August,
weakest late spring

Escarole

Year-Round
Best December through
April

Fava Beans

Spring
Peak late April through
May, available sporadically
to September

•

Fennel

Fall, Winter, Spring
Strongest October through
April, peaks November and
December, sold year-round

•

Figs

Summer
Late May through
September, peak mid-June
through early July and early
August through mid-
September

Galia Melons

Summer
Sold year-round, best July through September

•

Garlic

Year-Round
Harvests in June, July and August

•

Grapefruit

Fall, Winter, Spring
Year-round, strongest October through May

•

Grapes

Spring, Summer, Fall
Strongest May through October, sold year-round

Green Garlic

Spring
March through June

•

Green Onions (Scallions)

Year-Round
Most abundant May through June

•

Green Snap Beans

Year-Round
At their best early winter, early spring, early fall

•

Haricots Verts (French Green Beans)

Year-Round
Best February through November

•

Honeydew Melons

Summer, Fall
August to October

•

Horseradish

Year-Round
Most abundant spring and late fall

Kale

Year-Round
Strongest December through February

•

Kohlrabi

Summer
June through October, peaks June and July

•

Jicama

Year-Round
Strongest December through April

•

Kumquats

Fall, Winter, Spring
October to April, sweetest in March and April

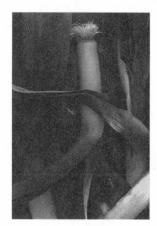

Leeks

Fall, Winter, Spring
Sold year-round, strongest late September through May

Lemons

Year-Round
Strongest April to June,
weakest July and August

•

Lettuce

Year-Round
Iceberg strongest April to
October; romaine strongest
early spring and mid-
autumn; Bibb best
June and July

•

Lima Beans

Summer, Fall
July through September,
into October

•

Limes

Year-Round
Strongest June through
August

•

Lobster
Mushrooms

Summer
Farmed year-round, wild
July and August

Mangoes

Spring, Summer
Strongest March through
August; flavor peaks in
August

•

Morel Mushrooms

Spring
Farmed year-round, wild
late March and April

•

Mustard Greens

Winter, Spring
Sold year-round, strongest
December through April,
weakest July and August

•

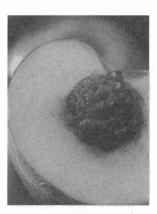

Nectarines

Summer
May to October, peak
August

•

Okra

Summer
Year-round, strong June
through October, peak July
and August

Onions

Year-Round
Most abundant August
to March

Oranges

Winter, Spring
November through May,
peak February through
April, sold year-round

•

Papaya

Year-Round
Most abundant April
through June and late
October through early
December

•

Parsnips

Fall, Winter, Spring
Best late September
through May

•

Peaches

Summer
May to mid-October, peak
late July through early
September

Pearl Onions

Summer, Fall, Winter

July through March

•

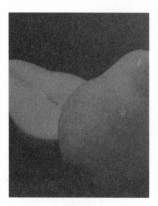

Pears

Fall, Winter, Spring

Anjou, October through May; Bartletts, late July through December; Bosc, August through April; Comice, August to March; Asian, late July through September

•

Persimmons

Fall, Winter

Domestic September through December, peak October; imports November to May

•

Pineapples

Year-Round

Hawaiian, year-round, peak April and May; Caribbean, December through February and August through September

Plums

Summer

Mid-May through mid-November, strongest mid-June through mid-August, peak July

•

Pomegranates

Fall, Winter

Late August to December, peak October

•

Porcini Mushrooms (Cepes, Boletus)

Spring, Fall

May through June, and October

•

Potatoes

Year-Round

Various harvests throughout the year

Pumpkin

Fall, Winter

October through December

Quince

Fall, Winter

September to January

Radishes

Spring

Sold year-round, peak March to May

•

Raspberries

Summer

May through November, strongest June through August

•

Rhubarb

Winter, Spring, Summer

January through August, peak April and May

•

Rutabagas

Year-Round

Strongest October through March

•

Shallots

Year-Round

Snow Peas

Year-Round

•

Spinach

Year-Round
Peaks December to May

•

Summer Squash

Spring, Summer
Sold year-round, peak April
through September

•

Strawberries

Spring
Sold year-round; California
harvests strongest March
through June, peak in April;
Florida harvests peak in
March; East Coast local
harvests mid-June through
early July

•

Sugar Snap Peas

Year-Round
Strongest February through
September

Sweet Onions

Spring, Summer
Best March through June,
some varieties into August,
other varieties late
December through March

•

Sweet (English or Green) Peas

Year-Round
Most abundant January
through June, peak May to
early June

•

Sweet Potatoes

Fall, Winter, Spring
Sold year-round, weakest
June through August

•

Swiss Chard

Spring, Summer, Fall
April through November,
strongest June through
October

•

Tangerines

Winter, Spring
November through March

Tomatoes

Year-Round
At their best July through
September

•

Turnips

Year-Round
Strongest October through
March

•

Turnip Greens

Fall, Winter, Spring
Strongest October through
March

•

Watermelons

Summer
Peak June through August;
sold year-round

Winter Squash

Summer, Fall, Winter
August through March,
peak October through
December

•

Yellow Wax Beans

Fall, Winter, Spring
October to June

Spring is a time for

the first **stalks** of asparagus

roasted lamb

baskets of strawberries

piles of fava beans

bushels of artichokes

brandied cherries

dark-green **bunches** of sorrel leaves

tender **shoots** of green garlic

salt-rubbed new potatoes

young, **tender** carrots

wild morel mushrooms

crisp green peas

the beginning of apricots,

a sign of **summer** fruits to come.

spring

Spring is a time for vegetable stews. This one, created by Times Staff Writer Russ Parsons, is extremely simple and designed to be adaptable to whatever vegetables you find fresh in the market. The vegetables are cooked separately in boiling water, allowing each to be cooked to its proper texture. You don't, for instance, want to overcook the potatoes. If your potatoes are walnut-sized and need no further trimming, be sure to cut a "belly band" around the middle, removing a thin strip of peel to keep the potatoes from bursting when they cook.

SPRING VEGETABLE STEW

Makes 6 Servings

1 POUND SUGAR SNAP PEAS

SALT

1 1/2 POUNDS SMALL WHITE BOILING POTATOES, CUT INTO WALNUT-SIZE PIECES

4 ARTICHOKES, OUTER PART TRIMMED, LEAVING HEART AND STEM ONLY

2 TABLESPOONS BUTTER

2 FRESH SHIITAKE MUSH-ROOMS, STEMS DISCARDED, COARSELY CHOPPED

1 BUNCH GREEN ONIONS, WHITE PARTS ONLY, CUT IN 1-INCH LENGTHS

1 HEAD ROMAINE LETTUCE, INTERIOR WHITE LEAVES ONLY, COARSELY CHOPPED

1 TEASPOON CHOPPED FRESH MINT

2 TABLESPOONS CHOPPED FRESH OREGANO OR MARJORAM

1/4 CUP CHOPPED FRESH PARSLEY

JUICE OF 1/2 LEMON

Cook sugar snap peas in large pot of rapidly boiling, lightly salted water just until bright green but still crisp, 30 to 45 seconds. Remove to mixing bowl full of ice water to set color.

Cook potatoes in same boiling water until barely tender, about 15 minutes. When done, remove from pan, salt lightly and drain on kitchen towel.

Add trimmed artichokes to boiling water and cook until just tender, about 15 minutes. Drain, remove fuzzy chokes with serrated grapefruit spoon and cut in eighths lengthwise. (Dish can be prepared to this point up to 4 hours in advance and refrigerated until almost ready to serve.)

Melt butter in large skillet or Dutch oven over medium-low heat. Add mushrooms and green onions and cook until onions soften, 15 to 20 minutes.

Add potatoes and artichokes and cook just until heated through. Add sugar snap peas and lettuce and cook just until lettuce wilts, about 5 minutes. Add mint, oregano and parsley and stir to mix well. Add lemon juice. Season to taste with salt. Do not cook too long or potatoes will begin to break down.

Each serving:
208 calories; 232 mg sodium; 10 mg cholesterol; 4 grams fat; 38 grams carbohydrates; 8 grams protein; 3.79 grams fiber.

spring

Turnips and peas, sweet and green as spring, are a perfect counterpoint to rosy slices of medium-rare leg of lamb.

The lamb is soaked overnight in a red wine marinade, and a quick stock is made from the hip bone and scraps. (Removing the hip bone before roasting the lamb makes the leg easier to carve.) You can make the stock as simple or as involved as you like. Times Staff Writer Russ Parsons simply roasted the bones until everything was nicely browned, then simmered the stock for an hour or so with root vegetables. If you want, you could just cook the lamb scraps in some diluted canned chicken broth.

ROAST LAMB WITH FRESH PEAS AND TURNIPS

Makes 6 Servings

1 (4- TO 6-POUND) LEG OF LAMB, HIP BONE REMOVED AND RESERVED

2 CLOVES GARLIC, MINCED

3 SPRIGS FRESH THYME, MINCED

SALT

FRESHLY GROUND PEPPER

3 CUPS RED WINE

6 LARGE TURNIPS, PEELED, QUARTERED AND TURNED, OR 24 SMALL TURNIPS, PEELED

2 ONIONS, QUARTERED

4 CARROTS, CUT INTO CHUNKS

3 POUNDS FRESH PEAS, SHELLED AND PODS RESERVED

BUTTER

1 SHALLOT, MINCED

2 COARSE OUTER LEAVES ROMAINE LETTUCE, CUT IN THIN STRIPS

1/2 TEASPOON FRESH THYME LEAVES

Carefully trim away tough outer layer of fat (fell) from lamb. Rub lamb with garlic, thyme and salt and pepper to taste. Place in large plastic food bag. Pour wine over and seal tightly. Marinate, refrigerated, overnight, turning occasionally to coat lamb evenly with wine.

Meanwhile, roast reserved hip bone and any lean trimmings in greased roasting pan at 450 degrees until well browned. Cook turnips in rapidly boiling water just until knife easily pierces center, about 5 minutes. Remove from pan and refresh in ice water.

Place hip bone and trimmings, 1 quartered onion and 2 chopped carrots in medium saucepan. Cover with water and bring slowly to simmer. Cook, keeping at bare simmer, at least 1 hour. When done, strain and chill.

Next day, remove lamb from marinade, reserving marinade, and pat meat dry with paper towels. Place lamb on rack in greased roasting pan and scatter remaining onion and carrots around bottom of pan. Roast lamb at 325 degrees until internal temperature reaches 135 degrees. Allow 20 to 25 minutes per pound. When lamb is done, remove from roasting pan and place on serving platter or carving board loosely tented with foil to keep warm, at least 30 minutes.

While lamb is roasting, remove stock from refrigerator, skim fat and return to simmer along with handful of reserved pea pods and any reserved turnip peels. Cook at least 30 minutes.

In large sauté pan, combine peas, cooked turnips, 1/4 cup butter, shallot, lettuce, thyme leaves and 1/4 cup lamb stock. Place over medium heat and cook just until peas are no longer starchy.

While peas are cooking, remove onions and carrots and skim fat from meat juices left in roasting pan. Place pan over high heat and add reserved red wine marinade. Cook, scraping bottom, until marinade reduces to several tablespoons, 5 to 10 minutes. Add 1 cup lamb stock and cook until reduced to thin sauce. Keep warm.

When ready to serve, carve lamb (pouring juice into warm sauce) and place on platter. Bring sauce to boil and whisk in 2 tablespoons butter. Strain sauce into gravy boat and serve peas and turnips alongside lamb.

Each serving:
747 calories; 308 mg sodium; 144 mg cholesterol; 39 grams fat; 39 grams carbohydrates; 42 grams protein; 4.92 grams fiber.

If you can find walnut-sized baby turnips, turning—the technique of carving vegetables into uniform shapes and sizes—isn't necessary. To turn the vegetables, cut each large turnip into quarters, then turn each quarter into a shape roughly resembling a semi-deflated football—remove the hard lines, starting with the core and finishing with the two edges.

You certainly won't taste peas and turnips in the lamb sauce, though there is a slight vegetal sweetness. At the same time, some of the lamb stock goes into the peas and turnips. Again, you don't taste lamb, but there is a little bit of a dark undertone to the vegetables' bright flavors.

As for the lettuce cooked with the peas, the slightly bitter herbal flavor of the leaves really makes the taste of the peas come alive.

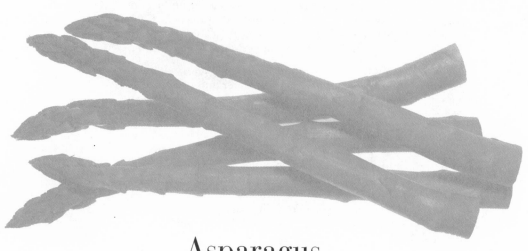

Asparagus

Above all others, asparagus is the vegetable we most associate with spring. It's the first green vegetable that gives relief from winter produce, and when it's cheap and abundant, we can't get enough.

Of course, the best way to eat it is blanched and served with sweet butter and maybe a squeeze of lemon juice.

It also can be baked, served cold as a salad with vinaigrette, stewed with other vegetables to make a soup or ragout, grilled over coals, cooked in risotto, baked in a tart or folded into an omelet.

It adapts comfortably to the different flavors of herbs and oils, including olive, peanut, sesame and walnut oils. It's terrific, for instance, tossed with peanut oil, diced shallots and parsley. Another of our favorite ways to serve it: drizzled with brown butter and scattered with shaved Parmesan cheese and a grinding or two of black pepper. For a richer version using the same flavors, broil cooked asparagus with butter and Parmesan or other kinds of cheese.

•

Quite a lot is made about the proper way to cook asparagus; there are special pans that allow the tougher stem ends to be submerged in the boiling water while the tender tips are merely steamed. But asparagus also cooks quite well in either a large kettle or skillet of boiling water. Don't worry too much about the tough parts—just break off the fibrous ends beforehand and peel the thicker stalks.

GRILLED ASPARAGUS WITH EGG-AND-CAPER SAUCE

Makes 4 to 6 Servings

Cookbook author Deborah Madison devised this recipe, which at heart is simple asparagus in vinaigrette, but more substantial with just a few more flavors—from the grilling, from the capers, from the richness of the hard-boiled egg. If possible, use thick asparagus. The stalks need to cook very slowly over a medium-low fire in order to be thoroughly done.

EGG-AND-CAPER SAUCE

2 HARD-BOILED EGGS

1/4 CUP EXTRA-VIRGIN OLIVE OIL

2 TO 3 TABLESPOONS TARRAGON OR CHAMPAGNE VINEGAR

2 TABLESPOONS CAPERS, RINSED

1 LARGE SHALLOT, FINELY DICED

SALT

FRESHLY GROUND PEPPER

FINELY CHOPPED CHERVIL OR PARSLEY

ASPARAGUS

2 POUNDS THICK ASPARAGUS

SALT

LIGHT OLIVE OIL

RED MUSTARD LEAVES, OPTIONAL

EGG-AND-CAPER SAUCE

Chop boiled egg whites and yolks separately. Combine chopped egg whites and yolks, oil, vinegar, capers and shallot in bowl. Season to taste with salt, pepper and chervil. Toss gently. Yolks and oil will gradually emulsify to give sauce body.

ASPARAGUS

Break off tough ends of asparagus and trim ends evenly. Parboil in boiling salted water about 1 minute. Rinse in cold water to stop cooking and drain. Brush stalks lightly with olive oil. Season to taste with salt.

Grill stalks over slow fire or in grill pan over medium-low heat, turning asparagus to cook evenly on all sides. (To test for doneness, pierce stalks with sharp point of knife—they should be firm, but knife should penetrate easily.)

Arrange grilled asparagus on platter or individual plates lined with red mustard leaves. Ladle Egg-and-Caper Sauce over asparagus and serve.

Each of 6 servings:
149 calories; 134 mg sodium; 71 mg cholesterol; 14 grams fat; 4 grams carbohydrates; 4 grams protein; 1.20 grams fiber.

*With the abun-
dance of spring-
time asparagus,
good cooks often
turn to soup. In
this one, cookbook
author Deborah
Madison pairs
asparagus with
fresh peas in a
vegetarian stock
enriched by leeks
as well as the
stems and pods of
the asparagus and
peas. Two hand-
fuls of sorrel melt-
ed with leeks taste
wonderful with
the rest of the
vegetables, though
they do give the
soup a slightly
dingy, army-green
color. If you'd like
to keep the soup a
brighter green,
omit the
sorrel during
cooking, but add a
few leaves at the
end to garnish.*

ASPARAGUS AND PEA SOUP

Makes 6 Servings

1 POUND THIN ASPARAGUS, TRIMMED

4 SMALL LEEKS, WHITE PARTS ONLY (ABOUT 8 OUNCES WHEN TRIMMED)

1 QUART WATER

SALT

1 POUND SWEET PEA PODS OR 1 1/2 CUPS FROZEN PEAS

5 SPRIGS PARSLEY

3 TABLESPOONS BUTTER

2 HANDFULS SORREL LEAVES, STEMS REMOVED, LEAVES SLICED, OPTIONAL

3 TABLESPOONS FLOUR

2 CUPS MILK

1/2 TO 1 CUP HALF AND HALF OR WHIPPING CREAM, OPTIONAL

SEVERAL FRESH BASIL OR SORREL LEAVES, FINELY SLICED; THINLY SLICED ROUNDS OF CHIVES AND BLOSSOMS; OR CHOPPED CHERVIL

Cut top third of asparagus diagonally into thirds. Coarsely chop remaining stems and reserve for stock.

Cut 3 inches off top of trimmed leeks and coarsely chop. Reserve bottom part.

Bring water to boil and add salt to taste. Add diagonal-cut asparagus and blanch until nearly tender, about 2 minutes. Remove with slotted spoon, rinse in cold water and set aside.

Shuck peas, reserving shucked pods for stock. Blanch peas in same boiling water used to blanch asparagus, about 1 minute. Remove with slotted spoon, rinse in cold water and set aside.

Using same vegetable water, add asparagus stems, chopped leeks, pea pods and parsley sprigs (if using frozen peas, add 1/3 cup of them as well). Reduce heat and simmer 20 minutes. Strain broth and set aside.

Thinly slice reserved leeks and rinse well. Melt butter in saucepan. Add leeks and 1/2 teaspoon salt. If using sorrel, add now. Cook gently until leeks and sorrel begin to soften, about 5 minutes, then stir in flour. Mix well, then whisk in strained stock. Bring to boil, then simmer 20 minutes, stirring occasionally to make sure flour doesn't stick to bottom of pan. Purée soup in blender until smooth.

Return mixture to saucepan and add milk, blanched asparagus and peas. Cook just until soup is hot. Adjust seasonings. If necessary, thin soup with additional stock or water, or stir in half and half or cream to enrich. Garnish with fresh herbs.

Each serving:
199 calories; 315 mg sodium; 27 mg cholesterol; 9 grams fat; 23 grams carbohydrates; 9 grams protein; 4.82 grams fiber.

Spring begins for tens of thousands of Iranian Americans— and for many people throughout Iran, Central Asia and India—with the celebration of Nouruz. The Persian New Year's festival goes back at least 2,500 years when followers of ancient Persia's Zoroastrian faith marked the arrival of the spring equinox. Today's festival has evolved into a two-week period of feasting. Many of the foods eaten at this time are full of the symbolism of springtime and new life.

Spring herbs— which can include wild greens such as shepherd's purse and clover—give a fresh and unusual flavor to Nouruz ravioli (kok chuchwara), which is eaten in Central Asia during the holiday. Times Staff Writer Charles Perry translated this recipe from an anonymous Uzbek recipe. For convenience, you could use won ton wrappers rather than make your own noodle paste squares. But they come in the package dusted with cornstarch, so moisten the edges with some beaten egg to seal.

NOURUZ RAVIOLI
(KOK CHUCHWARA)

Makes 6 Servings

NOODLE PASTE SQUARES

2 CUPS FLOUR

1 EGG

1 TEASPOON SALT

RAVIOLI

1/2 CUP PLUS 2 TABLESPOONS BUTTER

1/2 POUND ONIONS, FINELY DICED

1 BUNCH GREEN ONIONS, FINELY CHOPPED

2 POUNDS MIXED SPRING GREENS, SUCH AS MINT, CILANTRO, CRESS, SORREL, CLOVER, SHEPHERD'S PURSE AND WILD SPINACH, ALL FINELY CHOPPED

2 TEASPOONS SALT PLUS EXTRA FOR PASTA WATER

GROUND CAYENNE PEPPER

NOODLE PASTE SQUARES

Combine flour, egg and salt in bowl. Knead hard 10 minutes. Cover with plastic wrap. Let stand 30 minutes. Roll out to even thickness and cut dough into 2-inch squares.

RAVIOLI

Melt butter in wide pan over low heat. Remove 2 tablespoons melted butter and keep warm on stove. Add diced onions to remaining 1/2 cup butter and sauté until tender. Add green onions, mixed greens, salt and 2 teaspoons cayenne.

Cook until greens are tender and reduced in size. Remove greens and reduce pan liquid by at least half. Mix reduced liquid into cooked greens.

Set out Noodle Paste Squares. Place filling in center of 1 square. Lightly moisten square's edges with water. Fold square diagonally over filling to make triangle, pinch edges to seal, then fold opposite corners of triangle over each other and pinch together. Continue with remaining squares until all filling is used.

Cook ravioli in boiling salted water until done, 3 to 4 minutes. Using slotted spoon or colander, remove and drain ravioli. Place in warmed serving bowl. Toss with reserved 2 tablespoons melted butter. Season to taste with cayenne.

Each 4-ravioli serving:
564 calories; 2,130 mg sodium; 132 mg cholesterol; 30 grams fat; 60 grams carbohydrates; 12 grams protein; 2.94 grams fiber.

Fava Beans

When ancient Greeks and Romans talked beans, they were talking fava beans. Medieval Englishmen who said something wasn't "wurth a bene" meant favas too. Probably Jack's beanstalk was a fava beanstalk too.

Of course, the magic may be in their disappearing act: Fava beans are the incredible shrinking vegetable. Start out with three pounds of whole pods and by the time you're done shucking and skinning, you wind up with 1 3/4 cups of usable beans. (That's if you have the willpower to keep from eating the sweet beans as you go.)

Certainly you need to remove the tough outer husk, but what about the thin skin surrounding each individual bean? It all depends on how old the favas are and how long they'll be cooked.

Young beans less than half an inch long with bright green skin can be eaten with the skins on after being cooked only 5 to 10 minutes.

When they are between a half-inch and three-fourths of an inch in length and their skins begin to turn opalescent, beans should be peeled if they are going to be cooked longer than 10 minutes.

Beans bigger than that should definitely be peeled and will develop a rich, meaty taste if cooked for 15 minutes.

It's a rare and puzzling thing, but for a few people, eating too many fresh fava beans can be poisonous. This genetically transmitted condition—called, appropriately, favism—was recognized only at the turn of this century and has been explained fully just in the last decade. Most of us, however, can eat as many favas as we can peel and eat.

CREAMED FAVA BEANS AND BACON

(FÈVES AU LARD FUMÉ)

Makes 4 Servings

5 POUNDS FAVA BEANS, IN PODS

1/4 POUND LEAN BACON

1 TABLESPOON BUTTER

1 BRANCH FRESH SAVORY (OR PINCH FINELY CRUMBLED DRIED SAVORY)

3 TABLESPOONS WATER

SALT

1/2 CUP WHIPPING CREAM

3 EGG YOLKS

FRESHLY GROUND BLACK PEPPER

LEMON JUICE

CHOPPED PARSLEY

Shell beans and remove skins from all except those pods that are tiny and bright green.

Cut bacon in 1/2-inch sections and parboil few seconds to remove excess salt and drain.

Cook bacon in butter in heavy saucepan over low heat 2 to 3 minutes. Bacon should remain limp. Add fava beans, savory, just enough water to moisten lightly and salt to taste. Cover tightly and cook over high heat a few seconds. Turn heat to low again so beans stew in their own steam rather than boil. Cook, shaking pan gently from time to time, until tender, 15 to 20 minutes. Remove from heat and cool 1 minute or so.

Mix cream, egg yolks and pepper to taste and stir gently into fava beans. Return to low heat, stirring until sauce is only lightly bound, coating spoon thinly. Sauce should not approach boil. Squeeze in few drops lemon juice to taste, sprinkle with chopped parsley and serve.

Each serving:

488 calories; 283 mg sodium; 267 mg cholesterol; 31 grams fat; 34 grams carbohydrates; 19 grams protein; 1.69 grams fiber.

Fava beans don't get any richer than this, and they don't get any more delicious, either. This recipe, adapted from Richard Olney's "Simple French Food" (Atheneum, 1974), is almost compulsively edible. After all, how bad can bacon, cream and egg yolks be?

Two of the most inconvenient foods you'll run across are fava beans and shrimp. But they're worth the trouble to prepare, especially when combined in this ragout created by Times Staff Writer Russ Parsons. The flavor of the fava beans complements the shrimp almost perfectly, and the jade and pale coral of the main ingredients make a striking presentation. The dish is actually quite easy to make. You may spend an hour peeling and chopping, but when it comes time to serve, you just heat everything through.

RAGOUT OF SHRIMP AND FAVA BEANS

Makes 6 Servings

2 POUNDS SHRIMP, PEELED, SHELLS AND HEADS RESERVED

1 CUP WHITE WINE

3 CLOVES GARLIC, MINCED

1 CARROT, FINELY CHOPPED

1 TOMATO, PEELED, SEEDED AND CHOPPED

1 TEASPOON SALT

2 TABLESPOONS OLIVE OIL

3 POUNDS FAVA BEANS

1 TEASPOON THYME LEAVES

Rinse shrimp shells and heads well. Combine with wine, 2 cloves garlic, carrot and tomato in saucepan. Add water just to cover. Simmer over medium heat 45 minutes to 1 hour.

Combine shrimp meat, remaining 1 clove garlic, salt and olive oil in bowl. Stir well to coat. Marinate at least 1 hour.

Remove fava beans from pods, then cover beans with boiling water and let stand off heat 5 minutes. Dump into colander and cool with cold water. Use thumbnail or small knife to cut slit in 1 end of each bean; squeeze bean out of its peel into bowl.

Strain 2 1/2 to 3 cups simmered shrimp stock into wide, flat pan. Add beans. Bring to simmer over low heat, cooking beans just until heated through, 5 minutes.

When ready to serve, bring beans and shrimp stock to rapid boil and add marinated shrimp and thyme. Cook shrimp through, 3 to 5 minutes. Taste for salt and serve.

Each serving:
440 calories; 627 mg sodium; 228 mg cholesterol; 8 grams fat; 40 grams carbohydrates; 46 grams protein; 2.06 grams fiber.

Artichokes

Artichokes are relatively long-lived—they commonly spend six to eight years in the field. And they're quite productive. A single plant will bear as many as a dozen main stalks in a year, and each main stock will produce one primary bud (1 to 1 1/2 pounds), several secondary buds (about 1/3 pound) and many tertiary ones (the so-called "baby" artichokes).

Most people eat artichokes steamed. It's a familiar method and there's minimal preparation: You trim the top and the bottom with the slice of a knife, steam until the outer leaves easily pull away (15 to 40 minutes, depending on the size of the bud), then dig into the center of the bud with a grapefruit spoon to remove the choke (some people don't even bother with this step and let guests eat around the choke).

But if the only way you've eaten artichokes is steamed, you don't know what you're missing.

Try tossing whole trimmed baby artichokes in the bottom of the pan when you're roasting meat or chicken, the way you would throw in baby potatoes. Slow-cooked in pan juices, they come out tender and delicious.

Or fry baby artichokes—not with a heavy batter, but merely quartered and fried in hot olive oil. Sprinkle them with a little salt, add a squeeze or two of lemon juice and you've got something wonderful.

ARTICHOKE RISOTTO

Makes 6 Servings

4 ARTICHOKES

JUICE OF 1 LEMON

2 TABLESPOONS OLIVE OIL

2 CLOVES GARLIC, MINCED

1 1/2 CUPS ARBORIO RICE

1 QUART NONFAT CHICKEN STOCK OR 3 CUPS CHICKEN BROTH WITH 3 CUPS WATER, BOILING

1/4 CUP GRATED PARMIGIANO-REGGIANO CHEESE

SALT

FRESHLY GROUND PEPPER

Trim artichokes by pulling off any leaves clinging to stem and 2 outer rows of leaves around base. Holding artichoke in 1 hand and sharp paring knife in other, turn artichoke against knife, trimming away outer leaves from base, holding knife parallel to stem. When outer leaves have been trimmed to where pale green to yellow base shows, lay artichoke on side and cut away top of leaves, roughly where leaves swell out. With sharp paring knife, peel dark-green skin of artichoke from base to stem, exposing light-green flesh. Set artichoke heart upside down on flat cap and cut in quarters lengthwise. Trim away hairy chokes. Cut stems in 1/4-inch pieces and cut bases in 4 or 5 pieces. As each artichoke is cleaned and chopped, set in pan filled with water and juice of 1 lemon to prevent discoloration.

Combine oil and garlic in cold, broad, heavy-bottomed, high-sided nonreactive skillet. Drain artichokes and place in pan. Place pan over medium heat and cook until garlic is translucent, 3 to 5 minutes. Do not let garlic brown. Add rice and stir with wooden spoon until rice becomes opaque and shiny and you hear dry "singing" sound of rice against side of pan.

Add 1 cup boiling stock to pan and stir with wooden spoon. There will be much bubbling and hissing. Cook, stirring constantly, until rice is almost dry. You should be able to see bottom of pan without liquid when you stir. Add another cup of boiling stock and stir as before until rice swells and softens. Continue adding stock and stirring until risotto is very creamy but just short of soupy. Individual grains should have distinct bite.

Remove risotto from heat and add Parmigiano-Reggiano. Stir briskly and forcefully to increase creaminess. Season to taste with salt and pepper.

Each serving:
279 calories; 767 mg sodium; 3 mg cholesterol; 7 grams fat; 46 grams carbohydrates; 9 grams protein; 0.9 gram fiber.

Simplicity is vital to a dish like risotto. An artichoke risotto should taste of artichokes. If there are other flavors in the dish, they should bring out the flavor of the main ingredient and never fight with it. A light hand is so important that this risotto, devised by Times Staff Writer Russ Parsons, is best made with a diluted stock; full-strength broth would overwhelm the artichokes.

Strawberries

Strawberries are a remarkably erratic fruit. They can be wonderful one day and average the next. The experts say you can tell a good strawberry by its color—the more red the berry has, the better. But we've found that with many of the newer varieties being introduced in markets, looks are deceiving. You'll find some of those big blushing beauties practically bulletproof when you take a bite. The best way to buy strawberries is by tasting.

Once you get strawberries home, keep them cool. Berries are at their peak the moment they're picked. To maintain their quality, gently put strawberries in a container and cover them to keep the cold air from passing over them when they're refrigerated. And be sure to bring the berries to room temperature before you serve them—their flavor will be fuller. Of course, in a perfect world you wouldn't refrigerate strawberries at all. You'd polish them off before they needed storing.

OLD-FASHIONED STRAWBERRY SHORTCAKE

Makes 6 Servings

SHORTCAKE

2 CUPS FLOUR

1/4 CUP PLUS 1 TABLESPOON SUGAR

1 TABLESPOON PLUS 1/2 TEASPOON BAKING POWDER

6 TABLESPOONS BUTTER, CHILLED AND CUT INTO SMALL PIECES

3/4 CUP WHIPPING CREAM

2 HARD-BOILED EGG YOLKS, MASHED

2 TABLESPOONS MELTED BUTTER

FILLING

3 PINTS STRAWBERRIES, WASHED, HULLED AND HALVED OR QUARTERED (DEPENDING ON SIZE)

2 TABLESPOONS SUGAR

1 CUP WHIPPING CREAM

Shortcake

Sift flour, 1/4 cup sugar and baking powder into bowl. Add chilled butter pieces. Using fingertips, work butter quickly and lightly into flour until mixture is consistency of very fine crumbs of sand. Add cream and egg yolks and stir with fork until dough just comes together.

Turn dough out onto floured work surface and knead briefly, just until smooth dough forms. Do not overwork. Pat or roll out dough to 3/4-inch thickness. Using floured 2 1/2- or 3-inch cookie cutter, cut out 4 rounds of dough. Gather up dough scraps, reroll and cut out 2 more rounds.

Put rounds on lightly buttered baking sheet. Brush with melted butter and sprinkle with remaining tablespoon sugar. Bake on middle rack of oven at 375 degrees until biscuits are golden brown and firm to the touch, 12 to 15 minutes.

Filling and Assembly

Toss strawberries and sugar together in bowl.

Whip cream until soft peaks form, several minutes. Cover and refrigerate.

Transfer biscuits to cooling rack and cool 2 to 3 minutes.

Carefully split biscuits in half and set tops aside. Place bottoms on dessert plates and heap strawberries onto them. Generously spoon whipped cream over strawberries and replace biscuit tops. Serve immediately with any remaining whipped cream on the side.

Each serving:
642 calories; 421 mg sodium; 208 mg cholesterol; 44 grams fat; 57 grams carbohydrates; 8 grams protein; 0.96 gram fiber.

When New York chef Larry Forgione presented his take on strawberry shortcake to the late James Beard, the food guru pronounced: "There can be no dessert better, only fancier." After tasting Forgione's shortcake for ourselves, we had to agree. Perfect, ripe spring strawberries deserve a shortcake this wonderful. The secret: hard-boiled egg yolk mixed into the dough. The recipe comes from Forgione's cookbook "An American Place" (William Morrow, 1996). Though you can find out-of-season strawberries in the stores year-round, taste them before you serve them on this shortcake. If they're not full of flavor, the way they should be during the peak of their season, don't use them. Instead, choose a fruit that fits the season— either fresh or stewed with sugar.

STRAWBERRY PRESERVES

Makes 4 (8-ounce) Jars

2 POUNDS STRAWBERRIES

2 1/2 CUPS SUGAR

1/4 CUP LEMON JUICE (OR COMBINATION LEMON AND ORANGE JUICES)

Wash and hull strawberries. Pick out half, preferably largest and firmest, add 1 1/4 cups sugar and lemon juice and crush with fork in bowl. Add remaining sugar, stir well and add remaining whole hulled berries.

Place mixture in wide preserving pan over high heat. Cook, stirring, until mixture comes to full rolling boil. Transfer to mixing bowl and set aside, uncovered, overnight.

Next day, bring berry mixture to boil in wide preserving pan over high heat. Cook, stirring, until mixture jells. Ladle into sterilized 8-ounce glass jars to within 1/2 inch of top and cover with clean, new lids, screwing bands down tight.

Place jars in large kettle of boiling water and process 10 minutes. Remove from water and cool. Lids should not spring back when touched.

Each 1-tablespoon serving:
35 calories; 0 sodium; 0 cholesterol; 0 fat; 9 grams carbohydrates; 0 protein; 0.08 gram fiber.

Russ Parsons first tasted this dessert at a wine-tasting dinner cooked by Michel Richard, chef of Los Angeles' Citrus restaurant. When he tried to get the recipe from Richard, the chef shrugged and said, "It's just strawberries and wine." Parsons tried several times to recreate the dessert and finally succeeded, after getting inspiration from an extraordinary batch of Seascape berries.

The "soup" can be served on its own or, as Parsons suggests, with a scoop of vanilla ice cream and chewy almond cookies. The cookie recipe was adapted from the Sicilian cookie bocconotti di mandorla from Mary Taylor Simeti's "Pomp and Sustenance" (Alfred A. Knopf, 1989).

A rosé would work for this dish. Our preferences lean toward fresh, fruity red wines—light Pinot Noir and Zinfandel, new-style Chianti, almost certainly Beaujolais.

STRAWBERRY SOUP AND COOKIES

Strawberry Soup

Makes 6 Servings

1 BOTTLE LIGHT RED OR ROSÉ WINE

1 CUP SUGAR

1 (3-INCH) PIECE VANILLA BEAN

2 PINTS STRAWBERRIES, WASHED AND HULLED

VANILLA ICE CREAM

6 ALMOND COOKIES

Combine wine and sugar in large non-reactive metal bowl and whisk well to dissolve. Split vanilla bean in half and scrape seeds into wine mixture. Add bean.

Leaving smallest berries whole, cut larger berries into similar sizes. Add to wine combination and let marinate in refrigerator at least 2 hours, or overnight.

To serve, ladle berries and wine into bowls and serve with 1/4-cup scoop vanilla ice cream and almond cookie.

Each serving:
429 calories; 42 mg sodium; 15 mg cholesterol; 10 grams fat; 64 grams carbohydrates; 5 grams protein; 0.84 gram fiber.

Almond Cookies

Makes 3 Dozen Cookies

3 CUPS BLANCHED, PEELED WHOLE ALMONDS

2 CUPS SUGAR

1 TEASPOON VANILLA EXTRACT

3 EGG WHITES, WHIPPED TO SOFT PEAKS

Coarsely grind almonds in food processor fitted with metal blade. Spread almonds on jelly roll pan and heat at 350 degrees to slightly toast nuts, about 5 minutes. Return almonds to food processor with sugar and grind to fine powder. Add vanilla and pulse to mix well.

Whip egg whites to soft peaks. Add almond powder, stirring well to create thick paste. Break off walnut-sized pieces of dough and lightly roll into balls. Place at least 1 inch apart on lightly buttered and floured baking sheets. Bake at 350 degrees until lightly browned on top, about 10 to 15 minutes. Let cool on pan 10 minutes. Remove to wire racks to finish cooling.

Each cookie:
115 calories; 5 mg sodium; 0 cholesterol; 6 grams fat; 13 grams carbohydrates; 3 grams protein; 0.28 gram fiber.

Sorrel is a lemony herb that cooks down to a creamy, almost fluffy sauce when sautéed. Spoon the sauce over grilled fish, chicken, an omelet or over these couscous-stuffed grape leaves.

Serving sorrel sauce over stuffed grape leaves with a few boiled new potatoes is traditional in Central and Eastern Europe. What's untraditional is Times Test Kitchen Director Donna Deane's low-fat approach to the sauce. The tartness of sorrel leaves varies, so taste the sauce before you add sugar.

For best results, the stuffed grape leaves should be allowed to cool in the broth about 30 minutes, then refrigerated overnight or until serving time. This allows the rolls to firm up, making them easier to handle so they won't fall apart when served.

Fresh sorrel is often available in farmers markets at a reasonable price, but in a pinch you can use spinach. (If you use spinach, add lemon juice for tartness. Also, it won't be necessary to add sugar to the sauce.)

STUFFED GRAPE LEAVES WITH SORREL SAUCE

Makes 32 Grape Leaves

GRAPE LEAVES

NONFAT LOW-SODIUM CHICKEN BROTH
1/2 (10-OUNCE) BOX COUSCOUS
NONSTICK OLIVE OIL COOKING SPRAY
2 CLOVES GARLIC, MINCED
1 CUP MINCED BROWN MUSHROOMS
1/2 CUP MINCED CARROT
1/4 CUP MINCED GREEN ONIONS
1/4 CUP TOASTED PINE NUTS
2 TABLESPOONS MINCED DILL
1 TABLESPOON LEMON JUICE

SALT
1 (8-OUNCE) JAR WHOLE GRAPE LEAVES

SORREL SAUCE

1 POUND SORREL LEAVES OR SPINACH LEAVES
1 TABLESPOON BUTTER
1 TABLESPOON FLOUR
1/2 CUP NONFAT MILK
1 TEASPOON SALT
2 TABLESPOONS SUGAR, OR TO TASTE

GRAPE LEAVES

Bring 1 1/4 cups chicken broth to boil. Stir in couscous. Cover and remove from heat. Let stand 5 minutes. Fluff with fork.

Spray wok or skillet with olive oil cooking spray. Add garlic, mushrooms and carrot and sauté until mushrooms are tender, 2 to 3 minutes. Stir into couscous along with green onions, pine nuts, dill and lemon juice. Season to taste with salt.

Rinse grape leaves. Place 1 leaf, shiny side down, on counter. Snip off stem end. Spoon 1 generous tablespoon couscous filling onto grape leaf. Fold stem end of leaf over filling, then fold sides to center and roll up. Repeat with remaining grape leaves and filling.

Spray grill with nonstick olive oil and sear stuffed grape leaves on top of grill until lightly charred on all sides. Lightly spray grape leaves with olive oil cooking spray while cooking.

Line bottom of large pot with unstuffed grape leaves. Arrange browned stuffed grape leaves, seam side down, in pot. Add chicken broth or water to cover. Put inverted plate on top of grape leaves to hold them in place while simmering. Bring to simmer, cover and cook until tender, 35 to 45 minutes. Remove from heat. Let stand to cool to warm. Remove plate from pot. Carefully remove cooked grape leaves to platter for serving.

SORREL SAUCE

Wash sorrel and remove any tough stems. Coarsely chop leaves. Set aside.

Melt butter in large saucepan. Blend in flour until smooth. Cook and stir until flour turns medium brown. Stir in chopped sorrel. Cook and stir until leaves wilt and turn brownish green in color, about 2 minutes. Stir in milk. Heat to simmering and stir until sauce thickens, 2 to 3 minutes. Stir in salt and sugar to taste. To serve, spoon sorrel sauce over stuffed grape leaves.

Each stuffed grape leaf:
37 calories; 131 mg sodium; 1 mg cholesterol; 1 gram fat; 6 grams carbohydrates; 2 grams protein; 0.18 gram fiber.

Cherries

Few things can beat the explosive sweetness of a perfectly ripe cherry.

To get great cherries, pass up the cherry-red ones. Ripe cherries are dark red. It's not an accident that many cherry varieties include "black" in the name— Black Tartarians, Black Eagles and the rare Black Republicans.

Add a drop or two of almond extract to any recipe that includes cherries and you'll get a much deeper cherry flavor. That's not as odd as it seems: Some cherry liqueurs and most cherry flavorings come from almond pits. Go slow; 1/4 teaspoon of almond extract is enough to flavor a whole quart of cherry ice cream.

The addition of a little sweetish red wine vinegar also helps savory cherry dishes. Don't use an expensive one: What you're looking for is a combination of sweet and sour, not a strong wine flavor. Balsamic vinegar helps too, but it's not quite as true to flavor. In either case, the flavor of the vinegar should be almost subliminal. Add it very slowly and stop as soon as the dish acquires a slight tang.

BRANDIED CHERRY ICE CREAM

Makes 6 Servings

1 POUND CHERRIES, PITTED

1/2 CUP SUGAR

1/2 CUP BRANDY

2 CUPS MILK

3 EGG YOLKS, LIGHTLY BEATEN

1 CUP WHIPPING CREAM

1 TEASPOON VANILLA EXTRACT

DASH SALT

1/4 TEASPOON ALMOND EXTRACT

Combine cherries, sugar and brandy in medium mixing bowl, cover tightly and refrigerate overnight.

Drain cherry juice into small saucepan, reserving cherries. Over medium-high heat, reduce juice to syrup, about 10 minutes. Let cool.

Gently heat 1 cup milk and egg yolks, beating constantly, until mixture thickens. Stir cooked mixture into remaining milk, fold in whipping cream and chill. When ready to make ice cream, add reduced cherry syrup, vanilla, salt and almond extract and freeze in ice cream maker according to manufacturer's instructions. Midway through freezing, add brandied cherries.

Each serving:
350 calories; 101 mg sodium; 197 mg cholesterol; 19 grams fat; 30 grams carbohydrates; 6 grams protein; 0.13 gram fiber.

CHERRY-RED ONION MARMALADE

Makes 8 Servings

1/4 CUP CHICKEN STOCK

8 CUPS VERY THINLY SLICED RED ONIONS (ABOUT 2 LARGE)

1/4 CUP BALSAMIC VINEGAR

2 CUPS PITTED CHERRIES

SALT

FRESHLY GROUND BLACK PEPPER

Bring stock to boil in large pot and reduce by half over medium-high heat. Add onions, reduce heat to medium-low and cook, covered, until very soft, about 45 minutes. Uncover and continue to cook, stirring occasionally, another 30 minutes. Add vinegar and cherries and cook until caramelized, 45 minutes to 1 hour. Season to taste with salt and pepper.

Each 1/4-cup serving:
36 calories; 63 mg sodium; 0 cholesterol; 0 fat; 8 grams carbohydrates; 1 gram protein; 0.24 gram fiber.

Times Test Kitchen Director Donna Deane developed this recipe. The addition of just 1/4 teaspoon of almond extract has a remarkable effect on the flavor, making a very good thing even better.

Times Test Kitchen cook Mayi Brady came up with this recipe as an accompaniment to grilled veal chops. It's terrific with other grilled meats, too, and is especially good with pork tenderloin.

Summer is a time for

apricots fresh from the tree

peaches dripping with juice

eggplant grilled on the barbecue

roasted red peppers

buttered corn on the cob

hot blueberry buckles

ice cream-crowned plum tarts

sprigs of basil for everything

cool slices of watermelon

a chilly honeydew ice

the zucchini invasion

and, finally, the arrival of tomatoes

that taste the way tomatoes should.

summer

The appearance of apricots means that plums, peaches and nectarines will soon follow. In the meantime, enjoy this apricot-almond clafoutis developed by Times Staff Writer Russ Parsons.

The truly wonderful thing about this recipe is its adaptability. A clafoutis is just about the perfect way to present summer's soft fruits. Tweak the seasoning just a little bit, and the recipe can be made with cherries (substitute cherry liqueur or vanilla for the almond extract), peaches or nectarines (combine with raspberries instead of almonds) or plums (add a little ground clove, or maybe dust the top with cinnamon sugar).

What's more, you can't imagine anything easier. Essentially, this is a very eggy pancake batter that you simply pour over sliced fruit.

APRICOT-ALMOND CLAFOUTIS

Makes 6 to 8 Servings

SUGAR

3 EGGS

3/4 CUP WHIPPING CREAM

3/4 CUP MILK

1/2 TEASPOON ALMOND EXTRACT

1/2 CUP FLOUR

8 APRICOTS, ABOUT, CUT IN HALF AND PITTED

BUTTER

1/3 CUP SLIVERED ALMONDS

Place 1/4 cup sugar, eggs, cream, milk and almond extract in blender or food processor and blend until smooth. Sift flour over mixture and pulse just to mix. Set batter aside to stand 10 minutes.

Arrange apricots, cut-side down, in heavily buttered and sugared 9-inch glass pie plate. When batter has rested, pour batter over apricots. Sprinkle with almonds and 1 to 2 tablespoons sugar.

Bake at 400 degrees until puffed and brown, about 45 minutes. Serve immediately.

Each of 6 servings:
290 calories; 59 mg sodium; 142 mg cholesterol; 17 grams fat; 30 grams carbohydrates; 8 grams protein; 0.69 gram fiber.

Peaches and Nectarines

There may be no food experience quite so summery as biting into a perfectly ripe peach or nectarine and feeling the juice trickle down your chin.

Though peaches and nectarines are available through most of the hot weather months, it's important to remember that there are actually hundreds of varieties of both, each coming into season for only a two- to three-week period.

Peaches and nectarines ripen fairly well off the tree. Keep them at room temperature in a paper bag (it holds in the ethylene gas that speeds ripening). Check regularly to see if the color is right. If you miss a day, you risk an unpleasant peach surprise.

When buying peaches and nectarines, don't be fooled by the red blush. That is a characteristic of the variety and does not reflect ripeness. Instead, look at the paler background color. It should be golden, or at least creamy, when the fruit is ripe.

If you're going to use peaches and nectarines in desserts, peel them first. It's easy to do: Simply drop them in boiling water for 10 to 15 seconds. Take them out and dip them in ice water to stop the cooking. The skins should peel right off.

BAKED STUFFED NECTARINES

Makes 8 Servings

6 TABLESPOONS UNBLANCHED
WHOLE ALMONDS

8 AMARETTI (ITALIAN
MACAROONS)

6 TABLESPOONS BUTTER,
SOFTENED

1 1/2 TABLESPOONS SUGAR

1 EGG YOLK

1/2 TO 1 TEASPOON KIRSCH

1 1/2 POUNDS NECTARINES,
CUT IN HALF AND PITTED

1 TO 2 TABLESPOONS MELTED
BUTTER

Toast almonds at 350 degrees until sweet smelling, 6 to 7 minutes. Almonds should not brown inside. Chop almonds by hand into 1/8- to 1/4-inch chunks.

Crush amaretti between sheets of wax paper using rolling pin. Crumbs should be in tiny chunks, not fine powder.

Beat butter until light and fluffy. Add sugar, then egg yolk and continue beating until mixture is again light and fluffy. Beat in amaretti and almonds and flavor with kirsch to taste.

Scoop out enough flesh from pit of nectarine to make hole big enough to hold rounded tablespoon of filling. Arrange nectarines face-up in buttered baking dish. Brush tops of fruit with melted butter and bake at 375 degrees until filling has browned and nectarines are cooked through and tender, about 20 minutes. Cool 10 minutes or so, then when cool enough to handle, slip off skins. Serve warm.

Each serving:
274 calories; 111 mg sodium; 82 mg cholesterol; 19 grams fat; 25 grams carbohydrates; 4 grams protein; 0.89 gram fiber.

California has seen some exceptional peach and nectarine crops in recent years, and we've made all the usual peach and nectarine dishes: pie, cobbler, crisp, ice cream. One of our favorites is this very simple preparation from Lindsey Shere's "Chez Panisse Desserts" (Random House, 1985). It combines the flavors of nectarines, cherries (in the kirsch) and almonds, and even the amaretti are flavored with peach pits.

Cookbook author and Times columnist Marion Cunningham worries about the future of pie. She constantly meets people who are afraid to make pie because they fear the shame of tough crusts and watery or stodgy fillings. But follow her recipe and you'll make the perfect peach pie. Cunningham recommends using your hands to mix the flour and shortening, because your fingers will learn the right "feel" of the dough.

This makes one 8- or 9-inch pie. If you don't know the size of your pie pan, take a ruler and measure the distance from inside the top of the pan on one side to the opposite side. The pan should be about 1 1/2 to 1 3/4 inches deep.

FRESH PEACH PIE

Makes 6 to 8 Servings

PEACH FILLING

1 CUP SUGAR

1/4 CUP FLOUR

4 CUPS PEELED AND SLICED PEACHES

1 TABLESPOON LEMON JUICE

1/4 TEASPOON MACE OR GRATED NUTMEG, OPTIONAL

BASIC PIE DOUGH

2 CUPS FLOUR

1/2 TEASPOON SALT

2/3 CUP SHORTENING

1/2 CUP COLD WATER

2 TO 3 TABLESPOONS BUTTER, OPTIONAL

PEACH FILLING

Mix sugar and flour in large bowl. Add peaches, lemon juice and mace and toss well to combine.

BASIC PIE DOUGH

Mix flour and salt in large mixing bowl. Drop shortening in 1 chunk on top of flour mixture. Break chunk of shortening into 6 pieces and roll them around in flour mixture.

Dip hands into bowl and rub 1 chunk of shortening between thumb and fingers so that shortening and flour blend into little pieces. Let fall back into bowl. Keep going to bottom of bowl with your hands, gathering shortening and flour, rubbing and letting it drop back into bowl. Do this until mixture becomes small bits of shortening coated with flour. Size will not be uniform but will look like mixture of lentils and tiny peas.

Add water all at once by sprinkling. Stir with fork to incorporate water into mixture.

Generously flour work surface and hands. Scoop dough out of bowl, plop onto work surface and pat into rough ball. Divide in half.

Roll out half of dough into circle about 12 inches in diameter, lifting dough and sprinkling additional flour onto work surface as needed so that dough doesn't stick.

To transfer to pie pan, roll dough loosely around rolling pin and unroll, starting at far side of pie pan, so that dough drops into the pan. Drape dough onto bottom and sides of pie pan; avoid stretching dough. Let about 1 1/2 inches of dough hang over outer edge of pan. Pile Peach Filling onto dough. Put bits of butter over fruit. Roll out remaining dough for top crust and drape over pie. Trim away excess dough around edges but leave enough to tuck under top of pie pan edge. Crimp edges with fork or fingers and cut several vents in top.

Bake 10 minutes at 425 degrees, then reduce heat to 350 degrees and bake until juices bubble around edges on top of pie and crust is lightly browned, about 40 minutes more.

Each of 8 servings:
401 calories; 148 mg sodium; 0 cholesterol; 17 grams fat; 59 grams carbohydrates; 4 grams protein; 0.64 gram fiber.

Figs pose a practical problem for the cook because they contain an enzyme called ficin, which curdles milk and eventually turns it bitter. That didn't stop Times Staff Writer Russ Parsons from developing this ice cream, though. The figs and peaches, their perfume enhanced by a bit of amaretto, are heavenly when combined with cream—and eaten the same day, before the ficin works its mischief. But it's unlikely any of this delicious ice cream will be left over.

WHITE PEACH AND FIG ICE CREAM

Makes 8 Servings

2 WHITE PEACHES, PEELED

4 FRESH FIGS, PREFERABLY KADOTA (LIGHT GREEN), STEMS REMOVED

SUGAR

1 TABLESPOON AMARETTO OR ALMOND-FLAVORED LIQUEUR

1 1/2 CUPS WHIPPING CREAM

1 1/2 CUPS MILK

DASH SALT

Seed peaches and cube flesh, taking care not to bruise flesh. Coarsely chop figs.

Combine peaches, figs, 1 tablespoon sugar and amaretto in medium bowl. Cover with plastic wrap and chill at least 1 hour.

Combine cream, milk, 1/2 cup sugar and salt in another bowl. Cover with plastic wrap and chill at least 1 hour.

Combine fruit and cream mixture in container of ice cream maker and freeze according to manufacturer's instructions. Makes 1 quart.

Each serving:
272 calories; 58 mg sodium; 67 mg cholesterol; 18 grams fat; 26 grams carbohydrates; 3 grams protein; 1.31 grams fiber.

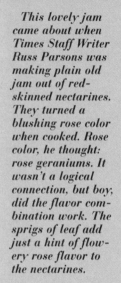

This lovely jam came about when Times Staff Writer Russ Parsons was making plain old jam out of red-skinned nectarines. They turned a blushing rose color when cooked. Rose color, he thought: rose geraniums. It wasn't a logical connection, but boy, did the flavor combination work. The sprigs of leaf add just a hint of flowery rose flavor to the nectarines.

NECTARINE AND ROSE GERANIUM JAM

Makes About 2 Cups, 2 to 3 (1/2-Pint) Jars

2 POUNDS SLICED NECTARINES **1/2 TEASPOON LEMON JUICE**

1 3/4 CUPS SUGAR **3 SPRIGS ROSE GERANIUM**

Bring nectarines and sugar to boil in large, flat pan, stirring constantly. Cook over medium-high heat until sugar is transparent and fruit is softened. Add lemon juice and stir well. Pour into large, flat dish and cool overnight.

Next day, ladle nectarine mixture into large saucepan and bring rapidly to boil, stirring frequently. Cook until liquid begins to fall away from metal spoon in thin sheet rather than steady stream, about 5 minutes.

Place rose geranium sprig in bottom of each of 3 sterilized 1/2-pint glass canning jars. Fill jars with jam, leaving about 1/2-inch head space.

Fasten with new lids and place in boiling water bath for 10 minutes. Remove and cool. Check lids by pressing down in center. Lid should not spring back; if lid springs back, return to water bath for 5 more minutes. Tighten lids and wipe clean. Store in cool, dark place.

Each 1-tablespoon serving:
55 calories; 0 sodium; 0 cholesterol; 0 fat; 14 grams carbohydrates; 0 protein; 0.11 gram fiber.

It's a cookie! It's a crisp! This exquisitely seasonal recipe from cookbook author and Times columnist Abby Mandel is like a fruit crisp with a chewy, cookie-like topping.

WARM PLUM AND RASPBERRY COOKIE CRISP

Makes 6 to 8 Servings

6 CUPS THINLY SLICED DARK-SKINNED PLUMS

2 TABLESPOONS WATER

2 TEASPOONS VANILLA EXTRACT

2 1/2 TEASPOONS QUICK-COOKING TAPIOCA

3/4 CUP GRANULATED SUGAR (1/4 CUP MORE IF PLUMS ARE SOUR)

3/4 TEASPOON CINNAMON

2 CUPS RASPBERRIES

1 EGG, SEPARATED

3/4 CUP DARK BROWN SUGAR, PACKED

1/2 CUP BUTTER, CHILLED, CUT INTO 8 PIECES

3/4 CUP FLOUR

PINCH SALT

STRAWBERRY OR VANILLA ICE CREAM OR FROZEN YOGURT, OPTIONAL

Combine plums, water and vanilla in 6-cup glass baking dish. Combine tapioca, granulated sugar and 1/4 teaspoon cinnamon in small bowl. Add to plums and toss until plums are well coated. Add raspberries and toss gently. Set aside.

Combine egg yolk, brown sugar, butter, flour, remaining 1/2 teaspoon cinnamon and salt in food processor and process until finely crumbed and just beginning to clump together. Do not overprocess.

Spoon topping evenly over fruit. Gently pat to cover, then press more firmly so topping adheres to fruit. Whip egg white until frothy and brush on crust.

Place baking dish on baking sheet to catch any drips. Bake at 375 degrees until top is very dark brown and juices are bubbling, 50 to 60 minutes. Cool at least 1 1/2 hours before serving. (Can be made a day ahead, cooled completely, covered and refrigerated. For serving, reheat, uncovered, at 350 degrees until warm, about 10 minutes.) Serve warm with scoop of vanilla or strawberry ice cream or frozen yogurt.

Each of 8 servings, without ice cream or yogurt:
390 calories; 151 mg sodium; 44 mg cholesterol; 13 grams fat; 69 grams carbohydrates; 3 grams protein; 4.38 grams fiber.

New England is home to a lot of comfortable, unpretentious fruit desserts that resemble pie but lack a bottom crust. Everybody loves cobbler and crisp; most people cringe at the idea of desserts named buckle and grunt. But it's hard to beat a good buckle.

In effect, a buckle is an upside-down cake with the fruit mixed into the batter and a crunchy streusel topping. The result is like a coffee cake full of fruit.

This buckle from "The Jordan Collection of New England Cookery" (Jordan Hospital Club, Plymouth, Mass., 1976) disappeared in The Times Test Kitchen within minutes of being baked. As for the odd name: In some recipes (though not this one), the fruit is arranged on top of the dough and sinks into it during baking. Possibly people thought a buckle looks as if it's buckling when this happens.

WILD BLUEBERRY BUCKLE

Makes 6 to 8 Servings

BUCKLE	1/2 CUP MILK
3/4 CUP SUGAR	2 CUPS BLUEBERRIES
1/4 CUP SHORTENING	STREUSEL
1 EGG	1/2 CUP SUGAR
2 CUPS FLOUR	1/2 TEASPOON CINNAMON
1/2 TEASPOON SALT	1/3 CUP FLOUR
2 TEASPOONS BAKING POWDER	1/4 CUP BUTTER

BUCKLE

Cream sugar and shortening by beating until fluffy. Beat in egg. Sift together flour, salt and baking powder and add to shortening alternately with milk. Blend in blueberries and pour into buttered and floured 10x6-inch baking dish.

STREUSEL

Combine sugar, cinnamon, flour and butter and sprinkle over top of buckle. Bake at 375 degrees until top is browned, about 45 minutes.

Each of 6 servings:
517 calories; 440 mg sodium; 58 mg cholesterol; 18 grams fat; 84 grams carbohydrates; 7 grams protein; 0.76 gram fiber.

Fourteen pints of berries cooked down into one dessert? Are we crazy? Yes, we're absolutely crazy. This recipe, from Buffalo Club Chef Patrick Healy, is the heady, concentrated essence of summer in a sophisticated gelatin. The terrine is a great way to make use of the berries available at farmers markets. It's visually stunning, too.

TERRINE OF SUMMER BERRIES IN NATURAL ASPIC

Makes 12 Servings

3 1/2 PINTS STRAWBERRIES, HULLED	WATER
3 1/2 PINTS BLACKBERRIES	1 1/2 CUPS SUGAR
3 1/2 PINTS BLUEBERRIES	1/2 CUP LEMON JUICE
3 1/2 PINTS RASPBERRIES	10 LEAVES SHEET GELATIN OR 2 1/2 (1/4-OUNCE) ENVELOPES UNFLAVORED GELATIN

Cut 3 pints strawberries in half. Slice remaining 1/2 pint strawberries.

Simmer halved strawberries, 3 pints blackberries, 3 pints blueberries, 3 pints raspberries, 1 cup water, sugar and lemon juice over low heat 20 minutes. Strain through cheesecloth.

Soak gelatin leaves in very cold water until soft, about 2 minutes. Squeeze out excess water. (If using powdered gelatin, follow manufacturer's directions.) Measure 1 quart hot berry juice and add gelatin. (Save excess berry juice for another use.) Cool to room temperature.

Combine remaining berries in terrine or mold. Pour room-temperature berry aspic over fresh berries and refrigerate until set, at least 4 hours or overnight.

To serve, put 1 tablespoon Yogurt Sauce on each dessert plate. Top with slice of berry terrine.

Each serving:
285 calories; 10 mg sodium; 0 cholesterol; 2 grams fat; 70 grams carbohydrates; 4 grams protein; 8.19 grams fiber.

YOGURT SAUCE

Makes 1 1/2 Cups

1/2 VANILLA BEAN	1 CUP YOGURT
1/4 CUP WHIPPING CREAM	MILK

Scrape seeds from inside of vanilla bean with point of sharp knife and add to whipping cream. Beat cream until whipped. Slowly whisk in yogurt. Add milk until desired consistency is reached.

Each 1/4-cup serving:
72 calories; 41 mg sodium; 19 mg cholesterol; 5 grams fat; 4 grams carbohydrates; 3 grams protein; 0 fiber.

Blackberry ice cream—oh, my. You can't go wrong. But you can do even better than ordinary blackberry ice cream by using crème fraîche. With its gentle tartness, it's more delicate than yogurt, more sophisticated than regular cream. This recipe, by Charity Ferreira of The Times Test Kitchen, makes the most luscious blackberry ice cream we've ever had.

Crème fraîche— thick, luscious, slightly tart—is the secret of many a French recipe. In France, you can find it anywhere. Here you'll have to go to an upscale market. Or you can make your own, as Charity Ferreira did in The Times Test Kitchen. It's absurdly easy. Use the extra to top any sliced summer fruit.

BLACKBERRY CRÈME FRAÎCHE ICE CREAM

Makes 7 Cups

2 PINTS BLACKBERRIES

1 1/2 CUPS PLUS 2 TABLESPOONS SUGAR

4 EGG YOLKS

2 1/2 CUPS MILK

2 CUPS *CRÈME FRAÎCHE*

Purée blackberries in food processor or blender. Add 6 tablespoons sugar and refrigerate.

Beat egg yolks with 1/2 cup plus 2 tablespoons sugar. Heat milk with remaining sugar, stirring until sugar is dissolved.

Whisk little of hot milk mixture into yolks, then whisk yolk mixture into rest of hot milk. Cook over low heat, stirring constantly, until slightly thickened. Stir in *crème fraîche* and refrigerate overnight.

Just before freezing, combine blackberry purée with custard mixture. Freeze in ice cream maker according to manufacturer's instructions.

Each 1-cup serving:
531 calories; 72 mg sodium; 247 mg cholesterol; 28 grams fat; 63 grams carbohydrates; 6 grams protein; 3.37 grams fiber.

CRÈME FRAÎCHE

Makes 5 Cups

5 CUPS HEAVY WHIPPING CREAM

5 TABLESPOONS BUTTERMILK

Warm cream to 100 degrees, or just above lukewarm. Remove from heat and stir in buttermilk. Transfer to clean plastic container. Allow mixture to stand, loosely covered, at warm room temperature until thickened, 12 to 36 hours. Stir and taste about every 8 hours. Final *crème fraîche* should have slightly tart flavor. Once thick, it can be stored in refrigerator up to 10 days.

In most vegetable stews, you start over high heat to brown the ingredients, then reduce it to marry them. But this delightful summer mélange starts low, with green onions, and the temperature goes up with every successive addition: zucchini, tomatoes and corn. Otherwise the zucchini would come out soggy and the corn raw.

As easy as this recipe is, Times Staff Writer Russ Parsons says there are a few things to remember. Don't add too much water—you want to steam the zucchini, not boil it. Don't be tempted to substitute stock—you want the fresh taste of the vegetables. Don't overdo the oregano. And stick with plum tomatoes—regular tomatoes may give off too much liquid.

SUMMER STEW

Makes 6 Main-Dish or 8 Side-Dish Servings

1 1/2 POUNDS SMALL ZUCCHINI	PEPPER
WATER	2 PLUM TOMATOES, SEEDED AND CHOPPED
1/4 CUP (1/2 STICK) BUTTER	
1 BUNCH GREEN ONIONS, WHITE PARTS ONLY, MINCED	2 EARS CORN, KERNELS ONLY
SALT	1/4 CUP CHOPPED MIXED HERBS (BASIL, PARSLEY, MARJORAM AND/OR OREGANO)

Trim ends of zucchini and rinse under cold water, rubbing to remove any loose dirt. Place in bowl of ice water and soak 15 minutes. Remove from water, cut in half lengthwise and slice 1/4 to 1/2 inch thick. Drain on paper towels.

Cook butter and green onions in large skillet over medium-low heat until butter is melted and onions are soft, about 5 minutes. Add zucchini and increase heat to medium. Season with salt to taste, and cook, stirring, until zucchini begins to look shiny, about 5 minutes.

Add 1/4 cup water and cook, stirring, until all liquid evaporates, 9 to 10 minutes. Zucchini should be somewhat soft. Season to taste again with salt and few grinds of pepper and increase heat to high. Add tomatoes and cook, stirring, until tomatoes melt into stew, about 5 minutes.

Add corn kernels and mixed herbs and cook, stirring, until corn is just cooked through, about 2 minutes. Remove from heat, adjust seasoning and serve.

Each side-dish serving:
112 calories; 136 mg sodium; 21 mg cholesterol; 8 grams fat; 10 grams carbohydrates; 2 grams protein; 0.79 gram fiber.

This simple, garlicky eggplant dish is common to some of the Tatar communities of Central Asia. It tastes fine as soon as it's made but gets even better in a couple of hours—the eggplant slices absorb whey from the yogurt, leaving it thicker and richer. The only sort of yogurt that will work is the plain, unflavored kind with no thickeners such as gelatin or tapioca (check ingredients list on carton). We learned of this recipe from an ethnic Tatar, Turan-Mirza Kamal.

EGGPLANT AND YOGURT
(PATLIJAN)

Makes 6 Servings

3 EGGPLANTS	**3 CUPS PLAIN YOGURT**
SALT	**3 CLOVES GARLIC, MINCED**
FLOUR	**PEPPER**
OIL FOR FRYING	**DILL**

Slice eggplants horizontally and sprinkle slices generously with salt. Place slices in mixing bowl and set bowl of same size or slightly smaller on top of slices. Put 2- to 3-pound weight in upper bowl and let eggplant sit 30 to 45 minutes.

Rinse salt from eggplant, drain and pat dry with paper towels. Dip slices in flour and fry in hot oil until golden. Drain on paper towels.

Mix yogurt and garlic. Spread some of yogurt mixture onto serving plate, cover with layer of eggplant slices, then layer of yogurt. Dust lightly with pepper and sprinkle with dill to taste. Repeat layering until eggplant is used up, ending with layer of yogurt. Let rest in cool place at least 2 hours before serving.

Each serving:
174 calories; 501 mg sodium; 14 mg cholesterol; 11 grams fat; 13 grams carbohydrates; 7 grams protein; 0.54 gram fiber.

RATATOUILLE

Makes 6 Servings

OLIVE OIL

1 YELLOW ONION, COARSELY CHOPPED

3 CLOVES GARLIC, MINCED

SALT

FRESHLY GROUND PEPPER

1 1/2 POUNDS EGGPLANT

3 RED BELL PEPPERS

3 SMALL ZUCCHINI, TO EQUAL 1 POUND, ENDS TRIMMED AND SOAKED IN COLD WATER 30 MINUTES

6 PLUM TOMATOES, PEELED, SEEDED AND CHOPPED

1 TABLESPOON BALSAMIC VINEGAR

3 TABLESPOONS ASSORTED FRESH HERBS (PARSLEY, THYME, BASIL, MARJORAM AND OREGANO)

Heat 1 tablespoon olive oil in medium nonstick sauté pan over medium-high heat. When hot, add onion and cook, stirring until translucent but not brown, 3 to 5 minutes. Add garlic and cook, stirring constantly, just until onion begins to brown. Do not let garlic brown. Season to taste with salt and pepper. Transfer to mixing bowl.

If using slender Asian eggplant, cut into quarters lengthwise and then into 1-inch sections, without peeling. If using round Italian eggplant, trim top and bottom, peel and cut into 1-inch dice.

Heat 1 tablespoon olive oil over medium-high heat in same sauté pan and add eggplant. Cook, stirring constantly, until eggplant begins to brown, about 5 minutes. Reduce heat to medium and continue cooking until eggplant is rather soft, about another 10 minutes. Season to taste with salt and pepper. Combine with onion and garlic in mixing bowl. If necessary, cook eggplant in 2 batches, using another 1 tablespoon oil.

Remove tops and bottoms of peppers, cut in half lengthwise and remove seeds and fibers. Cut into 1/2-inch strips lengthwise and then into 1-inch dice. Heat 1 tablespoon olive oil over medium-high heat in same sauté pan. When hot, add peppers and cook, stirring, until peppers become tender, 5 to 10 minutes. Season to taste with salt and pepper. Combine with onion and eggplant in mixing bowl.

Cut zucchini into quarters lengthwise and then into 1-inch sections. Heat 1 tablespoon olive oil over medium-high heat in same sauté pan and add zucchini, stirring constantly, until zucchini just begin to brown. Reduce heat to medium and cook until tender-crisp. Season to taste with salt and pepper. Combine with onion, eggplant and peppers in mixing bowl.

Increase heat to high and add tomatoes to sauté pan. Stir and add balsamic vinegar. Cook briefly, scraping bottom of pan to get up any brown bits. Pour over vegetables and stir to combine.

Empty contents of mixing bowl into large sauté pan and cook over medium-low heat until vegetables are cooked thoroughly. Onion, eggplant and peppers should be very soft, and zucchini should still have some bite. During last 5 minutes, add mixed herbs and stir well. Taste again. Adjust seasonings if necessary. Serve hot or at room temperature.

Each serving:
144 calories; 60 mg sodium; trace cholesterol; 9 grams fat; 15 grams carbohydrates; 3 grams protein; 2 grams fiber.

Few things match the taste of grilled meat quite as well as ratatouille. A little smoky, a little sweet, it has a melting tenderness that plays well against the crisp char of a good steak or grilled chicken. It's also the perfect clean-out-the-fridge food—the flavor mutates depending on the proportion of the vegetables. With a lot of zucchini, it will be firmer and sweeter. With more eggplant, it's softer and smokier. You can substitute different herbs with pleasant effect.

If you're in a hurry, cook the onions, then the eggplant, then the peppers, zucchini and tomatoes all in the same pot. But if you have the time, cook them separately and then combine for a final simmer. That way each vegetable keeps some of its identity, making for a more varied and colorful stew. This is Times Staff Writer Russ Parsons' recipe.

Fried zucchini flowers are one of the classic uses of pastella, *the Italian version of a flour-and-water batter. The mixture should be thin enough that it barely coats the flower; you should be able to see the orange of the petal through the crust. The flowers can also be fried without a filling.*

This version came about on a day when Times Staff Writer Russ Parsons was planning to serve a mozzarella salad as an appetizer and accidentally added too much garlic. Too strong by itself, its flavors were just right when encased in a fried flower.

STUFFED ZUCCHINI FLOWERS

Makes 8 to 10 Servings

1/2 POUND SMALL FRESH MOZ-
ZARELLA BALLS (BOCONCCINI,
CILIEGINI OR OVALINI)

2 CLOVES GARLIC, MINCED

1/4 TEASPOON RED PEPPER
FLAKES

2 TEASPOONS OLIVE OIL

SALT

FRESHLY GROUND BLACK
PEPPER

24 ZUCCHINI FLOWERS (ABOUT
1 POUND), PREFERABLY WITH-
OUT ZUCCHINI ATTACHED

2 CUPS FLOUR

WATER

OIL FOR FRYING

1 BUNCH ARUGULA

GRATED ZEST OF 1/2 LEMON

Cut mozzarella balls in half and combine with garlic, red pepper flakes, olive oil and salt and pepper to taste. Marinate at least 30 minutes.

Soak zucchini flowers in large bowl of cold water to clean and freshen. Remove, 1 at a time, and carefully open blossom with tip of finger. Gently place 1 mozzarella piece deeply into each blossom. Place on tray.

When all flowers are stuffed, whisk together flour and enough water (about 1/2 cup) in large bowl to make mixture thick as heavy cream.

Heat oil to 375 degrees. Dredge blossoms 1 at a time in flour-water mixture, turning flower so top seals. Immediately place in hot oil. Do not crowd pan. Cook until oil stops bubbling and flower begins to brown, 5 to 7 minutes. Turn and cook another 2 to 3 minutes, browning second side.

Remove from oil, drain well and place on baking sheet lined with oil-absorbent paper (brown paper bag works well). Salt lightly and keep warm in 200-degree oven until ready to serve.

Wash and dry arugula well. Place on serving platter. Place fried zucchini flowers on top and sprinkle with lemon zest.

Each of 8 servings:
213 calories; 174 mg sodium; 22 mg cholesterol; 9 grams fat; 26 grams carbohydrates; 10 grams of protein; 0.62 gram fiber.

OKRA SOUP
(SOPA DE QUIMBOMBO CON BOLAS DE PLATANOS)

Makes 5 to 8 Servings

1 POUND FRESH OKRA	1 CUP TOMATO SAUCE
1/3 CUP PLUS 1 TO 2 TABLE-SPOONS OLIVE OIL	4 CUPS CHICKEN BROTH
1 SPANISH CHORIZO, SLICED	1 CUP DRY WHITE WINE
1 ONION, FINELY CHOPPED	1 TABLESPOON WHITE WINE VINEGAR
1 GREEN BELL PEPPER, SEED-ED, CORED AND CHOPPED	SALT
3 CLOVES GARLIC, FINELY CHOPPED	1/2 TEASPOON FRESHLY GROUND BLACK PEPPER
	2 PLANTAINS

Rinse okra in cold water, dry well and cut crosswise into 1/4-inch pieces. Set aside.

Heat 1/3 cup olive oil over medium heat in Dutch oven or large saucepan. Add chorizo and cook until lightly browned. Add onion and bell pepper and cook until onion is translucent, about 5 minutes. Add garlic and cook 30 seconds. Add okra and cook 5 minutes. Add tomato sauce, chicken broth, wine, vinegar, 1 teaspoon salt and pepper. Reduce heat to low and cook until okra is tender, about 40 minutes.

Cut plantains in 2-inch pieces, leaving skin on. Cook in boiling salted water until tender, about 30 minutes. Drain, peel and mash plantains, or put through ricer. Stir in just enough of remaining olive oil for purée to stick together.

Form boiled, mashed plantains into marble-sized balls by rolling between both hands. Drop plantain balls into soup just before serving and simmer just until warmed through, 3 to 4 minutes.

Each of 8 servings:
262 calories; 970 mg sodium; 7 mg cholesterol; 14 grams fat; 24 grams carbohydrates; 7 grams protein; 1.08 grams fiber.

Pasadena restaurateur Xiomara Ardolina shared this wildly delicious soup from her native Cuba. Many people recoil from okra because of its sliminess, but Ardolina says if you dry the pods carefully after washing them, then wipe the knife between slicing each pod, slime will not appear. Buy Spanish chorizo at Cuban markets or grocery stores that carry Latino products, or substitute a high-quality pork sausage.

If you don't have perfect tomatoes, Alice Waters recommends roasting them to a confit with oil and basil. Of course, as with most of her recipes, the better the original ingredient, the better the dish. We tried this recipe from "Chez Panisse Vegetables" (HarperCollins, 1996) with excellent farmers market tomatoes and with everyday tomatoes from the supermarket. The supermarket tomatoes came out good, but the farmers market tomatoes were amazing.

The tomato confit can be used in sauces or served as a side dish with meat or fish—or on pasta, as it is here. Another good idea: Smear a bit of the confit on crostini spread with goat cheese. This recipe adjusts easily up or down. Figure on two tomatoes and 3 to 4 ounces of pasta per person. You might also try roasting a few cloves of garlic with the tomatoes.

PASTA WITH TOMATO CONFIT

Makes 4 Servings

1 TO 2 BUNCHES BASIL LEAVES
8 TOMATOES
SALT
FRESHLY GROUND BLACK PEPPER

EXTRA-VIRGIN OLIVE OIL
ABOUT 1 POUND PASTA, SHAPE OF CHOICE

Make bed of basil leaves in bottom of oven-proof dish that will hold tomatoes snugly in 1 layer.

Peel and core tomatoes and place core-side down on basil. Lightly season with salt and pepper to taste. Pour in enough olive oil to come halfway up sides of tomatoes. Bake at 350 degrees until tomatoes are soft and lightly caramelized and have infused oil with their perfume, about 1 1/2 hours.

When tomatoes are nearly done, cook pasta in boiling, salted water just until tender, 8 to 10 minutes for most shapes. Drain pasta and place in serving bowl.

Remove tomatoes from oven, season with salt and pepper to taste and serve spooned over cooked and drained pasta.

Each serving:
592 calories; 98 mg sodium; 0 cholesterol; 16 grams fat; 97 grams carbohydrates; 17 grams protein; 1.94 grams fiber.

One reason we love simple, peas-anty dishes like polenta is that they can be dressed up so boldly. In this vegetarian recipe, fresh goat cheese and slightly charred red bell peppers provide a tangy sweetness that contrasts nice-ly with the creamy, rosemary-scented soft polenta. If you like, sprinkle the dish with black peppercorns crushed with the side of a knife.

The only problem with polenta is that most recipes call for continuous stir-ring, but Charity Ferreira of The Times Test Kitchen found that polenta doesn't suffer from a little neglect. As long as you give it several vigorous stirrings during the 20- to 25-minute cooking time, it leaves you free to do other tasks.

POLENTA WITH PEPPERS AND GOAT CHEESE

Makes 4 Servings

SALT

WATER

1 1/2 CUPS MEDIUM- OR COARSE-GROUND POLENTA

2 TEASPOONS OLIVE OIL

2 RED BELL PEPPERS, CUT INTO SMALL STRIPS OR PIECES

3 TABLESPOONS BUTTER

2 TABLESPOONS CHOPPED ROSEMARY

2 OUNCES GOAT CHEESE

FRESHLY GROUND BLACK PEPPER

2 TEASPOONS BALSAMIC VINEGAR

Add salt to taste to 7 cups water in large pot and bring to boil. Pour polenta into water in slow, steady stream, whisking contin-uously. Lower heat, cover and simmer until texture is smooth, rather than grainy, 20 to 25 minutes. Remove lid and whisk vig-orously 3 to 4 times as it cooks.

While polenta is cooking, heat olive oil in skillet until it smokes. Add bell pepper strips and cook, stirring once or twice, until skins are slightly charred and peppers are just barely soft, 3 to 5 minutes.

When polenta is done, stir in butter and rosemary. Pour polenta into 4 shallow bowls and distribute bell peppers and goat cheese over top. Sprinkle with black pepper to taste and drizzle with balsamic vinegar.

Each serving:
312 calories; 304 mg sodium; 39 mg cholesterol; 16 grams fat; 38 grams carbohydrates; 7 grams protein; 1.06 grams fiber.

When Test Kitchen Director Donna Deane found both fresh soybeans and fresh limas at the farmers market, she decided to make a healthy low-fat summer salad. Soybeans are high in protein, so there's no need to add fat by using meat or cheese. And lemon juice, garlic, anchovies and good ripe tomatoes give this salad all the flavor it needs—no need for a high-fat dressing.

As the soybeans cook, check periodically to be sure they are covered with water. Also taste to check for doneness. Because they're being used in a salad, they should be tender yet firm enough to hold their shape. If you can't find fresh soybeans, they're sold frozen in most Japanese markets.

FARMERS MARKET SALAD

Makes 16 Servings

1/2 POUND FRESH OR FROZEN SOYBEANS

1 POUND FRESH LIMA BEANS

1 RED ONION, MINCED

2 CLOVES GARLIC, MINCED

1 CUP CHOPPED CELERY

1/2 CUP CRUMBLED FETA CHEESE

1/4 CUP LEMON JUICE

1 (2-OUNCE) CAN ANCHOVIES, DRAINED AND MINCED

6 PLUM TOMATOES, DICED

1 BUNCH WATERCRESS

8 KALAMATA OLIVES

Cook soybeans in boiling water to cover until tender but still slightly firm, 30 to 35 minutes. Skim off any foam. Drain and rinse under cold water. Cool.

Rinse limas well, place in 2-quart saucepan and add water to cover. Bring to boil. Reduce heat and simmer 35 to 40 minutes. Skim off any foam. Drain and rinse under cold water. Cool.

Toss together cooked soybeans, lima beans, red onion, garlic, celery, feta cheese, lemon juice, anchovies and tomatoes.

Remove tough stems from watercress and stir into salad. Chill until serving time. When ready to serve, spoon onto platter and garnish with Kalamata olives.

Each serving:
81 calories; 222 mg sodium; 5 mg cholesterol; 3 grams fat; 9 grams carbohydrates; 6 grams protein; 1.13 grams fiber.

CORN AND SHRIMP SOUP

Makes 4 Servings

3 EARS YELLOW CORN

1 TABLESPOON BUTTER

1/2 CUP FINELY CHOPPED ONION

1 CLOVE GARLIC, MINCED

2 TEASPOONS GRATED GINGER ROOT

1/2 CUP MINCED RED BELL PEPPER

4 CUPS CHICKEN STOCK

1 POUND LARGE SHRIMP, PEELED AND DEVEINED

SALT, PEPPER

2 TABLESPOONS MINCED CHIVES

Cut kernels off cob and "milk" cob by running flat of knife down cob. Reserve kernels and "milk" together.

Melt butter in large pot over medium heat and add onion and garlic. Cook 5 minutes. Add ginger root and 1/4 cup bell pepper and cook another 5 minutes. Add corn and cook until corn begins to soften, about 5 minutes. Add stock and cook 10 minutes.

Remove 2 cups soup and purée in blender or food processor until smooth. Return to pot and bring soup to simmer. Add remaining 1/4 cup bell pepper and shrimp. Cook just until shrimp is pink and opaque, 3 to 4 minutes. Season with salt and pepper to taste. Garnish with minced chives.

Each serving:
241 calories; 1,037 mg sodium; 160 mg cholesterol; 7 grams fat; 18 grams carbohydrates; 30 grams protein; 0.74 gram fiber.

Mexican food, like Southern food, has the rap of being exactly what vegetarians and fitness buffs should avoid. But that doesn't apply to this salsa from vegetarian and fitness buff Lydia Estrella, who serves it at a meal of tofu enchiladas. It's an ultra-quick sauce, so it would be foolish to try to save time by making it ahead—avocado flesh discolors if exposed to air too long.

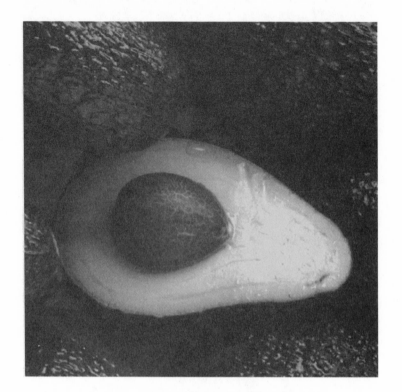

AVOCADO SALSA

Makes 6 to 8 Servings

2 AVOCADOS, DICED

1 TOMATO, DICED

1/2 SMALL ONION, DICED

1 TO 2 SERRANO CHILES, CHOPPED

SALT, PEPPER

Combine avocados, tomato, onion and chiles in bowl. Season to taste with salt and pepper. Stir to combine. Serve at once.

Each of 6 servings:
112 calories; 59 mg sodium; 0 cholesterol; 10 grams fat; 6 grams carbohydrates; 2 grams protein; 1.52 grams fiber.

END-OF-SUMMER SHRIMP STEW

Makes 4 Servings

2 TABLESPOONS OLIVE OIL

3 CLOVES GARLIC, CHOPPED

6 SMALL RED BOILING POTATOES, CUT INTO 1/3-INCH CUBES

1 CUP CHICKEN OR VEGETABLE STOCK

1 TEASPOON LIME ZEST, CHOPPED

1 TABLESPOON LIME JUICE

1 SPRIG THYME

1/2 JALAPEÑO, SEEDED AND MINCED

1/2 POUND GREEN BEANS, CUT INTO 1/2-INCH LENGTHS

KERNELS FROM 2 EARS CORN

6 PLUM TOMATOES, SEEDED AND CUT IN 1-INCH CHUNKS

SALT

CAYENNE PEPPER

1 POUND LARGE SHRIMP, PEELED AND DEVEINED

1/4 CUP CHOPPED PARSLEY

Heat olive oil in 4-quart saucepan. Add garlic and potatoes and stir over medium-high heat until potatoes are well-coated with oil. Continue cooking about 3 minutes. Before garlic turns color, add stock, lime zest and juice, thyme and jalapeño. Cover and simmer until potatoes are somewhat cooked but still crisp, about 5 to 7 minutes. Add green beans and simmer, covered, about 3 more minutes. Add corn and tomatoes and simmer, covered, another 3 minutes. Check broth for flavor. Add salt and cayenne to taste. Add shrimp and simmer until cooked through, 3 to 5 minutes. Serve immediately, dividing evenly among 4 bowls. Sprinkle with chopped parley.

Each serving:

266 calories; 424 mg sodium; 140 mg cholesterol; 10 grams fat; 24 grams carbohydrates; 24 grams protein; 1.66 grams fiber.

Hot-weather stews aren't impossible. Consider this one from frequent Food section contributor Michelle Huneven. It takes less than 20 minutes on a hot stove and makes use of the last of the summer garden (or farmers market) harvest. It's a fine way to bid farewell to fresh ripe tomatoes, corn on the cob and green beans. Although this recipe calls for large shrimp, if you don't mind all the peeling and deveining, you may use medium shrimp, which are less flashy to look at but just as tasty. (Be sure to shorten the cooking time to 2 to 3 minutes if you use smaller shrimp.)

Times Staff Writer Russ Parsons adapted this recipe from a dish served at Echo, a restaurant in Fresno, Calif., where partners Tim Woods and Adams Holland treat the local San Joaquin Valley produce simply and with respect. The syrup is flavored with mint and grated lime zest, which adds another dimension to the melons. Mix two or three melon varieties for an assortment of colors, flavors and textures.

The peeling method described works well for firm melons. With riper, softer melons, cut thin slices with the rinds attached, stack several slices and slice through to separate the peel from the flesh. If your melons are extremely sweet, decrease the sugar to 1/2 cup; if they're on the bland side, increase to 3/4 cup.

SLICED MELONS IN LIME-MINT SYRUP

Makes 8 to 10 Servings

2 CUPS WATER

2/3 CUP SUGAR

2 TO 3 SPRIGS MINT

GRATED ZEST OF 1 LIME

2 1/2 POUNDS ASSORTED MELONS

Heat water and sugar to boiling in small saucepan. Whisk until sugar is completely dissolved and remove from heat. Add mint sprigs and lime zest and let stand until cool. Strain through coffee filter into lidded jar, cover and chill. Makes 2 cups syrup.

Cut melons in half and remove seeds. Place each half cut-side down on cutting board and slice off top inch. Cut away peel with sharp knife, working down melon in 2- to 3-inch strips until melon is completely peeled. Cut each half in quarters, then cut in thin, 1/4-inch slices. (Melons will keep, tightly covered and refrigerated, about 2 hours.)

When ready to serve, arrange variety of melons in large deep platter. Pour syrup over and serve.

Each of 10 servings:
83 calories; 8 mg sodium; 0 cholesterol; 0 fat; 21 grams carbohydrates; 1 gram protein; 0.33 gram fiber.

*Honeydew com-
bines with fresh
lime juice and
Japanese honeydew
melon liqueur in
this quick, refresh-
ing nonfat ice. The
melon liqueur
smooths out the ice,
adds sweetness and
gives it a bright
green color.
Depending on the
sweetness of the
fruit, you may want
to add more or less
sugar to your taste.
This recipe, devel-
oped by Times Test
Kitchen Director
Donna Deane, takes
only about 30 min-
utes from start to
finish.*

HONEYDEW ICE

Makes 4 Servings

**3 CUPS PURÉED HONEYDEW
MELON**

**1 1/2 TABLESPOONS LIME
JUICE**

1 1/2 TABLESPOONS SUGAR

**1/2 CUP HONEYDEW MELON
LIQUEUR**

4 SLICES LIME, OPTIONAL

**4 SLICES BLOOD ORANGE,
OPTIONAL**

4 SPRIGS MINT, OPTIONAL

Combine honeydew purée, lime juice, sugar and liqueur. Freeze
in ice cream maker according to manufacturer's instructions. (If
making ahead, spoon finished ice into chilled loaf pan, cover and
freeze. Remove from freezer 10 to 15 minutes before serving.)

Spoon into serving glasses and garnish each with slice of lime
and slice of blood orange. Top with sprig of mint.

Each serving:
203 calories; 14 mg sodium; 0 cholesterol; 0 fat; 20 grams carbohydrates; 1 gram protein; 0.88 gram fiber.

Fall is a time for

the **scent** of ripe pears

the crisp **crunch** of apples

baskets of cranberry beans

candy-**sweet** dates

baked persimmons

butternut squash soup

bowls full of **fresh** walnuts

spicy pumpkin pie

sage **wisely** used

braised parsnips

red roasted beets

jewel-box-like pomegranates,

bursting with tart ruby seeds.

Is this a stew, a soup or a pasta? Who cares? This recipe, from Times Staff Writer Russ Parsons, is a perfect meal for a fall day when made with fresh cranberry beans, and it works fine in winter using dried beans. In a pinch, you could even substitute well-drained canned beans. Charring the tomatoes gives a slight smoky quality to this stew and intensifies the tomato flavor as well. You don't need to push the idea too far—just let the tomatoes scorch enough to flavor them.

STEW OF CHARRED TOMATOES AND CRANBERRY BEANS

Makes 4 Servings

3 PLUM TOMATOES	1 POUND CRANBERRY BEANS, SHELLED (ABOUT 1 1/2 CUPS)
2 OUNCES PROSCIUTTO, MINCED	WATER
1 TABLESPOON OLIVE OIL	SALT
1 CARROT, DICED	1/2 POUND DRIED PASTA SHAPES, LIKE GNOCCHI OR MEDIUM SHELLS
1/2 ONION, DICED	
1 CLOVE GARLIC, MINCED	2 TABLESPOONS TORN BASIL LEAVES
1 SMALL SPRIG SAGE	

Slice tomatoes in half lengthwise and place cut-side down on hot griddle. Cook until tomatoes begin to blacken and char, about 5 minutes. Turn over and repeat on opposite side, another 3 minutes. Cool, squeeze out seeds, chop and reserve.

Cook prosciutto in oil in large sauté pan over medium heat until lightly browned, about 5 minutes. Add carrot, onion and garlic, reduce heat and cook, covered, until vegetables soften, about 10 minutes.

Add sage, cranberry beans, tomatoes, 1 1/2 cups water and 1 teaspoon salt. Bring to boil, reduce to simmer and cook, covered, until beans are soft, about 30 minutes.

When beans are done, cook pasta in plenty of rapidly boiling salted water. Drain well and add to beans. Raise heat to high and cook, stirring, 2 to 3 minutes to meld flavors. Divide among 4 pasta plates and garnish with torn basil.

Each serving:
299 calories; 782 mg sodium; 8 mg cholesterol; 5 grams fat; 52 grams carbohydrates; 10 grams protein; 1.05 grams fiber.

Cesare Giaccone
works in an
impossibly tiny
restaurant in the
remote Italian
hamlet of
Albaretto Torre.
But he has been
called one of the
10 best chefs in
the world, and
food lovers eager-
ly make the drive
deep into the
Piedmont to sam-
ple his wares.
One day, Times
Restaurant Critic
S. Irene Virbila
walked in at
lunchtime to find
the grizzled
graphic designer
and wood-cut
artist Gianni
Gallo and a
friend hunched
over steaming
bowls of this
hearty bean soup.
When served, the
potatoes have
broken down to
small chunks, the
beans are plump,
tender and full of
flavor. Giaccone
doesn't cut the
pork riblets
apart. They're
meant to flavor
the broth.

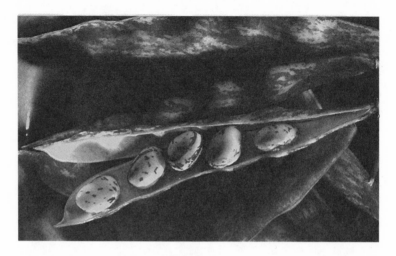

CRANBERRY BEAN SOUP WITH PORK RIBLETS

(ZUPETTO DI BORLOTTI)

Makes 6 to 8 Servings

1 POUND DRIED BORLOTTI OR CRANBERRY BEANS

WATER

EXTRA-VIRGIN OLIVE OIL

1 SMALL STALK CELERY, CHOPPED

1 SLENDER LEEK, CHOPPED

1 CLOVE GARLIC, CHOPPED

3/4 POUND SMALL BOILING POTATOES, PEELED AND QUARTERED

1 (2-INCH) STICK CINNAMON

1 SPRIG ROSEMARY

2 TO 3 SPRIGS PARSLEY

1/4 TO 1/2 POUND LITTLE PORK RIBS

SALT

FRESHLY GROUND BLACK PEPPER TO TASTE

Soak beans overnight in water to cover. Drain and cover with 2 quarts cold water. Bring slowly to boil.

Meanwhile, heat 2 tablespoons olive oil in skillet and sauté celery, leek and garlic until wilted. Stir into soup pot. Add potatoes, cinnamon, rosemary, parsley and pork ribs. Cook until beans are very tender, about 2 hours. Season with salt and pepper to taste. Serve in warmed soup bowls. Pass olive oil on side.

Each of 6 servings:
377 calories; 74 mg sodium; 7 mg cholesterol; 8 grams fat; 59 grams carbohydrates; 20 grams protein; 2.50 grams fiber.

LIMA BEAN AND SPINACH SALAD

Makes 6 Servings

BLUE CHEESE VINAIGRETTE

1/4 CUP OLIVE OIL

2 TABLESPOONS CIDER VINEGAR

2 TABLESPOONS LEMON JUICE

1/2 CUP CRUMBLED BLUE CHEESE

SALT, PEPPER

SALAD

1 1/2 POUNDS FRESH LIMA BEANS OR 1 (10-OUNCE) PACKAGE FROZEN

6 HARD-BOILED EGGS

1/2 CUP SLICED GREEN ONIONS

1 CUP SLICED CELERY

1/4 CUP CHOPPED DILL PICKLES

1/2 POUND SLICED BACON, COOKED AND CRUMBLED

1 (6-OUNCE) PACKAGE BABY SPINACH

2 CUPS SLICED ICEBERG LETTUCE

BLUE CHEESE VINAIGRETTE

Combine olive oil, vinegar, lemon juice, blue cheese and salt and pepper to taste. Makes about 3/4 cup vinaigrette.

SALAD

Shell lima beans and cook in boiling salted water to cover until tender, about 15 minutes. If using frozen beans, cook according to package directions. Let cool.

Chop 4 hard-boiled eggs. Combine limas, green onions, chopped eggs, celery, pickles and bacon, reserving small amount of bacon to sprinkle over salad, in serving bowl. Add spinach and lettuce and toss. Add Blue Cheese Vinaigrette and toss. Slice remaining 2 hard-boiled eggs and use to garnish salad.

Each serving:
395 calories; 759 mg sodium; 239 mg cholesterol; 28 grams fat; 16 grams carbohydrates; 20 grams protein; 1.64 grams fiber.

Times Test Kitchen Director Donna Deane developed this hearty yet light salad to go with the kind of party food she grew up with in Wisconsin: bratwurst marinated overnight with beer and onions and then grilled and served with sauerkraut. Fresh lima beans are available in summer and early fall; they're much better, in our opinion, than frozen or dried. Hard-boiled eggs, crumbled bacon and a blue cheese vinaigrette give the lima beans plenty of punch.

Pomegranates

Intensely perfumed and tart-sweet, pomegranate seeds contain the very snap of fall. But they don't yield their virtues easily. Obtaining the crunchy, crimson, tear-shaped seeds is pretty messy. It helps to pull the fruit apart underwater in a pot or basin. You can then work the seeds free (they'll sink while the pith or membrane floats) without turning your clothes red.

Pomegranate juice is difficult and time-consuming to extract but worth the effort, especially if you have a surplus of backyard fruit. (California grows the great majority of the nation's pomegranates, and many backyards have a thriving tree or two.) Five to six pomegranates yield 1 cup of juice.

In the fall, it's possible to find fresh pomegranate juice at farmers markets or advertised in the classified sections of rural newspapers. Fresh pomegranate juice is wonderfully complex, at once sweet and puckery, intense and wine-like; it makes an excellent base for gelatins, sorbets and ice cream, or it can be reduced to a sweet, full-bodied syrup for pancakes, drinks or basting.

Here are two methods for making fresh pomegranate juice, both splattery, so use gloves.

Method 1: Roll a whole pomegranate on a counter until it is soft as a ripe persimmon. Then cut the fruit open and squeeze the juice through a sieve into a bowl.

Method 2: Cut the fruit in half and remove the seeds. Place the seeds in a cheesecloth and squeeze out the juice with gloved hands.

Pomegranate juice can be boiled down to a concentrate known as pomegranate syrup or molasses. It's a traditional Middle Eastern sauce with a sharp, clear, fruity flavor that wakes up everything it touches—salads, meat, poultry, fish. And it's simple to make. Middle Eastern cooks reduce the juice without adding a thing; with our sweeter American pomegranates, it's necessary to add a cup of lemon juice and a cup of sugar to 6 cups of fresh or bottled pomegranate juice (it should reduce to about 2 cups molasses). Pomegranate molasses is also sold bottled in Middle Eastern markets as *dibs rummân* or *rob-e anâr*.

RIBS BASTED WITH POMEGRANATE AND RED PEPPER SAUCE

Makes 2 Main-Course or 4 Appetizer Servings

2 RACKS OF LAMB OR PORK BACK RIBS, APPROXIMATELY 1 POUND EACH, CUT INTO SEPARATE RIB PIECES

WATER

1 STICK CINNAMON, OPTIONAL

5 WHOLE CLOVES, OPTIONAL

3 TO 5 WHOLE ALLSPICE, OPTIONAL

1/4 CUP POMEGRANATE MOLASSES

1/4 CUP RED PEPPER SAUCE

2 TABLESPOONS OLIVE OIL

1 TABLESPOON LEMON JUICE

SALT

FRESHLY GROUND PEPPER

Place ribs in stockpot. Cover with water. Add cinnamon, cloves and allspice and bring to boil. Reduce heat and simmer 1 hour.

Combine pomegranate molasses, red pepper sauce, olive oil, lemon juice and salt and pepper to taste.

Remove ribs from water, drain and place in roasting pan. Season with salt to taste. Brush on pomegranate sauce. Bake at 300 degrees, basting every 20 minutes or so until caramelized but not dry, about 1 hour.

Each appetizer serving:
557 calories; 251 mg sodium; 90 mg cholesterol; 48 grams fat; 14 grams, carbohydrates; 17 grams protein; 0 fiber.

Pomegranate molasses combined with Middle Eastern red pepper sauce (which is really more like a paste) makes a terrific marinade for meats. Frequent Times Food section contributor Michelle Huneven put the two together to create this rib recipe, which was voted one of the Top Ten Food section recipes of 1995. The first bite of these ribs invariably provokes a response along the lines of "Oh! Tart!" But wait. Soon enough, the very tartness will prove addictive. The red pepper sauce is sold bottled in most Middle Eastern grocery stores.

ROASTED BEET SALAD WITH PICKLED ONIONS

Makes 4 Servings

1 RED ONION	NONSTICK OLIVE OIL SPRAY
1/2 CUP RICE VINEGAR	1 HEAD GARLIC
1 TEASPOON BALSAMIC VINEGAR	KOSHER SALT
1/4 CUP SUGAR	CRACKED BLACK PEPPER
1/2 TEASPOON SALT	1/4 YELLOW BELL PEPPER, MINCED
2 BUNCHES (ABOUT 1 3/4 POUNDS EACH) BEETS, WITH TOPS	

Peel onion and slice paper-thin. Combine rice vinegar, balsamic vinegar, sugar and salt in nonreactive bowl. Add sliced onion, cover and refrigerate overnight.

Cut tops off beets, leaving about 2 inches of stem. Spray baking pan with nonstick olive oil spray. Add beets and whole head garlic. Lightly spray vegetables with olive oil spray, then season with kosher salt to taste. Roast at 450 degrees until beets are fork-tender, 45 to 60 minutes. Remove garlic after about 30 minutes of roasting (it should be soft and lightly browned).

Remove beets from oven and let stand until cool enough to handle, about 20 minutes. Cut beets into 1/2-inch slices.

Drain onion, reserving vinaigrette. Squeeze garlic out of cloves, coarsely chop, then add to vinaigrette. Set aside.

Remove large stems from beet greens. Cut leaves crosswise into 1-inch strips. Spray large wok or skillet with nonstick cooking spray, add greens and sauté just until tender, 4 to 5 minutes. Season to taste with kosher salt and cracked pepper.

To serve, divide greens among serving plates. Top with beets and drained pickled onion. Drizzle roasted garlic vinaigrette over all. Garnish with yellow bell pepper.

Each serving:
207 calories; 598 mg sodium; 0 cholesterol; 1 gram fat; 49 grams carbohydrates; 5 grams protein; 2.74 grams fiber.

ONION RINGS

Makes 8 to 10 Servings

3 OR 4 RED ONIONS, SLICED 1/4-INCH THICK

3 TABLESPOONS BALSAMIC VINEGAR

2 CUPS FLOUR

1 CUP CORNSTARCH

1 TABLESPOON BAKING SODA

1 TABLESPOON BAKING POWDER

1/2 TABLESPOON SALT PLUS EXTRA FOR SERVING

1 (12-OUNCE) BOTTLE DARK BEER, ICE COLD

SODA WATER, ICE COLD

OIL FOR FRYING

Marinate onions in balsamic vinegar 1 hour.

Mix flour, cornstarch, baking soda, baking powder and salt in large bowl placed on top of larger bowl filled with ice. Whisk in beer, then enough soda water to thin batter to point that it just coats spoon.

Heat oil for frying to 375 degrees. Keeping batter on ice, dredge onions in batter and fry until light brown, about 1 minute. Remove and drain on paper towels, salt lightly and serve immediately.

Each of 8 servings:
271 calories; 608 mg sodium; 0 cholesterol; 2 grams fat; 42 grams carbohydrates; 4 grams protein; 0.28 gram fiber.

Some of us are always on the look-out for good onion ring recipes. This is a great one. The batter puffs up to a crisp, golden crust with just the right crunch. And you can still taste the onions. The recipe comes from the chefs at Campanile, who often use it for their lunch menu.

"The important thing is to keep the batter iced," says co-owner Nancy Silverton, "as if you were doing tempura." The batter's consistency is also a factor; you want it thick, but not so thick that it will mask the flavor of the onion.

Squash

Hard-shelled or winter squashes look more like instruments of self-defense than like something to eat. This is unfortunate, because winter squash at its peak, October through December, is not only delicious, it's extremely easy to cook.

We like the creamier, more richly flavored squash—butternut, kabocha and carnival, for instance—rather than the more vegetal-tasting fibrous varieties. You should make up your own mind. Here is a list of the more usual varieties:

Acorn—Semi-smooth, rich, semisweet, semi-squashy. A middle-of-the-road squash.

Banana—A very large squash, often sold in pieces, semi-smooth and bland.

Butternut—Semi-fibrous, very sweet and nutty with just a hint of squashiness.

Carnival—Slightly fibrous, complex flavor, rich, sweet and earthy.

Delicata—Very smooth, very vegetal.

Golden Acorn—Semi-smooth, not very sweet, fairly squashy.

Golden Nugget—Very smooth, semisweet, not much squash quality.

Green-Striped Turban—Very smooth, fairly vegetal.

Kabocha—Fairly smooth, very sweet with a nice squashy edge.

Red Kuri—Semi-fibrous, less sweet and more strongly squashy than most.

Spaghetti—Stringy and fibrous, bland, slightly squashy.

Sugar Pumpkin—Semi-fibrous, very bland with a slight vegetal edge.

Table Queen—Smooth, like an acorn squash.

White Acorn—Semi-fibrous and very vegetal.

Cooking With Squash

For most dishes, you'll want to start with squash pulp. There are two ways to get this.

Method 1: Prick the skin of the squash all over with a sharp carving fork, then bake it at 400 degrees until it is soft.

Method 2: Cut the squash in half, placing it cut-side down on a jelly-roll pan or in a roasting pan, then add a quarter-inch or so of water before baking. We find squash cooks more quickly and more evenly using this method, but the flavor may be a tad less concentrated.

Once the squash is cooked through—about 30 to 40 minutes using Method 2, about 50 to 60 using Method 1, depending on its size—simply spoon the pulp away from the skin.

Now you can make a squash dish as basic or complicated as you like. Whip the pulp with a little butter (or a lot; it's up to you), and you've got a side dish that is perfectly wonderful just as it is.

When you've roasted winter squash, you can add broth and flavorings to make the purée into a soup. Or you can leave out the broth and use the purée as a ravioli filling. This recipe is from Times Staff Writer Russ Parsons.

SQUASH RAVIOLI IN SAGE BUTTER

Makes 6 Servings

SQUASH FILLING

2 CUPS ROASTED SQUASH PULP (PAGE 91)

5 SLICES PROSCIUTTO, CHOPPED

1/4 CUP FRESH BREAD CRUMBS

1/2 CUP GRATED PARMIGIANO-REGGIANO CHEESE

1 TEASPOON SALT

1 TEASPOON FRESHLY GROUND BLACK PEPPER

1 EGG

PASTA DOUGH

2 1/4 CUPS FLOUR, PLUS MORE FOR DUSTING

1 TEASPOON SALT

1 TABLESPOON OLIVE OIL

3 EGGS

SAGE BUTTER

1/2 CUP BUTTER

2 TEASPOONS SAGE, MINCED

FRESHLY GRATED PARMIGIANO-REGGIANO CHEESE

SQUASH FILLING

Mix squash, prosciutto, bread crumbs, Parmigiano-Reggiano, salt and pepper in bowl. Taste and adjust seasoning; there should be definite black pepper bite. Add egg and mix well.

PASTA DOUGH

Place flour, salt and olive oil in work bowl of food processor fitted with metal blade and pulse once or twice to combine. Add eggs and run until dough forms ball that rides around on top of blade. Remove from machine, wrap in plastic and set aside for 1/2 hour.

Divide dough into quarters and run 1 piece through manual pasta maker at widest setting to flatten. Dust lightly with flour, fold into thirds and run through machine again. Repeat, re-folding, until dough is satiny to touch, 4 or 5 times.

Dust dough lightly with flour and run through machine on middle setting. Dust again and run through machine on next-to-thinnest setting. Lay pasta sheet on counter, cover with damp tea towel and repeat using rest of dough.

Using 1 sheet at a time, place 2-teaspoon mounds of filling along sheet about 2 inches apart and about 1 inch from edge. Brush other half of sheet lightly with water and fold evenly over top of other half, covering mounds of filling. Press firmly around each filling mound, squeezing out as much air as possible and creating tight seal. Cut into individual ravioli with pasta cutter or knife. Repeat, using rest of pasta sheets.

Bring large pot of lightly salted water to rolling boil. Add ravioli, few at a time, making sure they don't stick together. Cook until ravioli float to surface, about 5 minutes. Ravioli may be cooked in 2 batches to prevent crowding.

SAGE BUTTER

While ravioli are cooking, melt butter with sage in large skillet over medium heat. As soon as butter is melted, remove pan from heat.

Drain ravioli and add to skillet. Toss to coat well with butter and divide among 6 plates. Dust lightly with grated Parmigiano-Reggiano and serve immediately.

Each serving:
457 calories; 1,262 mg sodium; 192 mg cholesterol; 25 grams fat; 43 grams carbohydrates; 15 grams protein; 0.69 gram fiber.

Our staff thought this winter squash purée, flavored with nutmeg and bal-samic vinegar, was even better than mashed potatoes. This recipe was developed by Times Staff Writer Russ Parsons.

Belgian-born chef Anne Bunch is known as the Garlic Queen because she puts the fragrant bulb in so many of her dishes. But not in the desserts and not in this soup, which is adapted from her otherwise appropriately named book "Dancing With Garlic" (Olive Press Publications, 1995). The bright, fruity pungency of the orange marmalade perfectly rounds out butternut squash's warm earthiness.

BALSAMIC SQUASH PURÉE

Makes 4 Servings

2 TABLESPOONS MINCED SHALLOTS

1/4 CUP BUTTER

3 TABLESPOONS BALSAMIC VINEGAR

2 CUPS ROASTED SQUASH PULP (PAGE 91)

1 TEASPOON SALT

FRESHLY GRATED NUTMEG

Cook shallots in medium saucepan with 1 tablespoon butter over medium heat until soft, about 3 to 5 minutes. Add vinegar, increase heat to high and cook until vinegar is reduced to syrup, another 3 to 5 minutes.

Combine squash pulp and salt in separate pan and cook over low heat until heated through, about 5 minutes. Cut remaining 3 tablespoons butter into small cubes, add to squash and beat until fairly smooth.

Divide squash mixture in half. Add half of squash mixture to balsamic syrup and stir to combine. Combine both halves of squash mixture and swirl together. Serve immediately, dusted with freshly grated nutmeg.

Each serving:
159 calories; 708 mg sodium; 31 mg cholesterol; 12 grams fat; 13 grams carbohydrates; 1 gram protein; 0.83 gram fiber.

BUTTERNUT SQUASH AND ORANGE SOUP

Makes 8 Servings

1 (2-POUND) BUTTERNUT SQUASH

2 1/2 CUPS STRONG VEGETABLE BROTH

1/4 CUP ORANGE MARMALADE

1/2 CUP HEAVY WHIPPING CREAM

SALT

Peel squash, halve and remove seeds. Cut into 1-inch chunks.

Bring vegetable broth to boil in large saucepan. Add squash, return to boil and cook until squash is soft, about 25 minutes. Drain squash, reserving broth.

Purée squash and marmalade in food processor. Add broth as needed to facilitate blending. Return to saucepan. Add cream and heat until almost boiling. Add remaining broth. Season to taste with salt.

Each 1/2-cup serving:
108 calories; 335 mg sodium; 21 mg cholesterol; 6 grams fat; 13 grams carbohydrates; 2 grams protein; 1.41 grams fiber.

In the 19th century, American gourmets argued over the relative merits of pumpkin and other winter squashes as pie filling. In our own time, the issue has been resolved by a compromise—the canned pumpkin pie purée most of us use is a mixture of pumpkin and other squashes such as Hubbard, though pumpkin gets all the credit. It has an excellent flavor, and there's no reason to confine it to pie. This recipe from Bistro Garden at Coldwater uses it in a light, spicy soufflé.

Mexico was the place where many squash varieties were developed in pre-Columbian times, and it's still a place that respects the pumpkin. This recipe, a favorite of the Mexican artist Frida Kahlo, comes from "Frida's Fiestas: Recipes & Recollections of Life with Frida Kahlo" by Guadalupe Rivera and Marie-Pierre Colle (Crown Publishing Group, 1994).

PUMPKIN SOUFFLE

Makes 8 Servings

3 EGG YOLKS

GRANULATED SUGAR

1 TEASPOON VANILLA EXTRACT

1 TEASPOON CINNAMON

1/4 TEASPOON NUTMEG

1/4 TEASPOON CLOVES

1/2 CUP FLOUR

1 CUP MILK

1 CUP CANNED PUMPKIN PURÉE, SOLID PACKED

5 EGG WHITES

PINCH SALT

BUTTER

POWDERED SUGAR, OPTIONAL

WHIPPED CREAM, OPTIONAL

Mix egg yolks with scant 1/2 cup granulated sugar, vanilla, cinnamon, nutmeg and cloves. Add flour gradually until mixture forms smooth paste.

Bring milk to boil in saucepan. Add flour mixture. Boil 1 to 2 minutes without stirring. Then begin stirring continuously and cook until paste leaves sides of pan. Remove paste from pan, place in mixer with dough hook attachment and mix 5 minutes. Add pumpkin purée and mix well. Remove paste from mixer and let cool.

Wash mixer bowl thoroughly and dry. Place egg whites, salt and 1/2 cup granulated sugar in mixer with whisk attachment and whip until stiff, glossy peaks form. Fold 1/3 egg-white mixture into pumpkin mixture, then fold in remaining egg-white mixture until lightly but well incorporated.

Grease 8 (6-ounce) souffle ramekins with butter and sprinkle with granulated sugar, shaking out excess. Spoon pumpkin batter into ramekins and bake at 375 degrees until puffy and slightly gold-brown, about 17 minutes. Sprinkle with powdered sugar and serve immediately with whipped cream if desired.

Each souffle without powdered sugar or whipped cream:
195 calories; 96 mg sodium; 108 mg cholesterol; 4 grams fat; 35 grams carbohydrates; 5 grams protein; 0.52 gram fiber.

PUMPKIN IN SYRUP

Makes 24 Servings

1 1/2 CUPS WATER

4 POUNDS PILONCILLO (MEXICAN BROWN SUGAR CONES) OR

10 1/2 CUPS DARK BROWN SUGAR, PACKED

1 (10-POUND) PUMPKIN

Combine water and piloncillo in saucepan. Cook over low heat, stirring often, to make syrup.

Peel pumpkin and cut in chunks. Remove fibers and seeds. Score pulp in diamond shapes. Arrange pumpkin chunks in large saucepan. Add syrup, cover and cook over medium heat, stirring occasionally, until pumpkin is well soaked in syrup and deep caramel color, about 2 1/2 hours.

Each serving:
266 calories; 20 mg sodium; 0 cholesterol; 0 fat; 69 grams carbohydrates; 1 gram protein; 1.25 grams fiber.

Walnuts are available year-round, so we don't think of them as a seasonal food. They really are, though. New-crop walnuts have a milky sweetness and delicacy unlike the more bitter, nuttier flavor walnuts start developing within a few weeks after being picked. Fresh walnuts are perfect for making sauces to go with seasonal fall vegetables, such as eggplants, fennel and strong-flavored members of the chicory family. This recipe comes from cookbook author Deborah Madison.

GRILLED VEGETABLES WITH WALNUT SAUCE

Makes 6 Servings

6 LONG JAPANESE EGG-
PLANTS, EACH CUT LENGTH-
WISE INTO 3 SLICES

2 BULBS FENNEL, CUT IN
1/4-INCH SLICES

OLIVE OIL

SALT

FRESHLY GROUND PEPPER

1 CUP WALNUT MEATS

1 SMALL CLOVE GARLIC

1/4 CUP FRESH BREAD CRUMBS

1 CUP BOILING WATER, ABOUT

2 TO 3 TEASPOONS WALNUT OR
VIRGIN OLIVE OIL

1/4 TEASPOON FENNEL SEEDS,
CRUSHED

Brush eggplants and sliced fennel lightly with olive oil. Season with salt and pepper to taste. Grill over medium heat until done, 5 minutes per side for eggplant, 5 to 7 minutes per side for fennel. Remove to tray and keep at room temperature.

Combine walnuts, garlic and bread crumbs in food processor and process briefly until texture of fine crumbs. While processing, gradually pour in about 3/4 cup water. Stop and scrape down sides. Add remaining water if needed for medium consistency. For thinner sauce add more water. Stir in walnut oil and fennel seeds. Season to taste with salt and pepper. Serve over grilled vegetables.

Each serving:
205 calories; 75 mg sodium; 0 cholesterol; 19 grams fat; 8 grams carbohydrates; 4 grams protein; 1.43 grams fiber.

WALNUT NUGGET COOKIES

Makes 40 Cookies

1 CUP WALNUT MEATS PLUS EXTRA 40 PIECES FOR GARNISH

1/2 CUP (1 STICK) BUTTER, AT ROOM TEMPERATURE

1 TABLESPOON WALNUT OIL

1/4 CUP GRANULATED SUGAR

1/4 CUP LIGHT BROWN SUGAR, PACKED

DASH SALT

1 TEASPOON VANILLA EXTRACT

1 1/4 CUPS UNBLEACHED ALL-PURPOSE FLOUR

VANILLA SUGAR OR POWDERED SUGAR

Chop 1 cup nuts by hand or in food processor until like coarse sand. If using food processor, do not process too long.

Cream butter and walnut oil until smooth. Gradually add granulated and brown sugars and salt, beating until well blended. Add vanilla. Stir in ground walnuts. Work in flour, little at a time, until mixed.

Divide dough into 2 pieces. On lightly floured board, roughly shape each piece into log. Wrap each log in plastic wrap. Shape dough with hands to make squarish log about 1/2 inch across each side. Refrigerate until hardened, about 30 minutes, or freeze.

Cut logs into thin squares and set on lightly greased baking sheets. Press small piece of reserved walnuts into center of each cookie. Bake at 350 degrees until lightly browned on top, 8 to 10 minutes. Carefully remove with spatula to cooling rack. Cookies will become firm upon cooling. Dust with vanilla sugar. Store in covered container.

Each cookie:
66 calories; 7 mg sodium; 6 mg cholesterol; 5 grams fat; 6 grams carbohydrates; 1 gram protein; 0.15 gram fiber.

Walnut cookies and pastries are welcome at any time of year, but they're never better than when made with new-crop walnuts. Deborah Madison, who grew up in a walnut orchard, also contributed this recipe, which reinforces the walnut flavor by using a mixture of butter and walnut oil as shortening. Note: Keep a vanilla bean or two in a canister of sugar to make vanilla sugar.

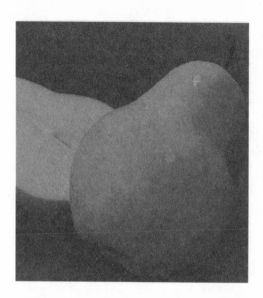

Pears

Unlike most modern fruits, which are genetic rats' nests of characteristics currently deemed desirable by agricultural marketers, most pear varieties have remained constant for decades and even centuries. When you pick up a ripe Bartlett or Anjou or Comice, you're getting much the same fruit someone was eating 200 years ago.

The Bartlett is the signature pear of California. It should be gold when ripe. Don't mind the russeting and brown spots it tends to acquire. It is the same pear as the Williams pear that dates to 18th-century England.

The Anjou, which is grown mainly in the Pacific Northwest, is the predominant commercial variety. It comes in green and red varieties and has a denser flesh than most pears. Seckels are tiny pears, perfect for spicing. Boscs have the familiar elegantly slim neck.

The queen of pears, though, is the Comice, so golden and rounded it almost resembles a quince. Formally called the Doyenne du Comice, it was developed in the mid-19th century in France's Loire Valley. Juicy, spicy and with melting flesh, it is truly a pear fit for royalty.

Another way pears are different from most other fruits is that they will only ripen after having been picked. This is one reason they often show up in stores slightly green. To finish ripening a pear, simply leave it at room temperature for a day or two.

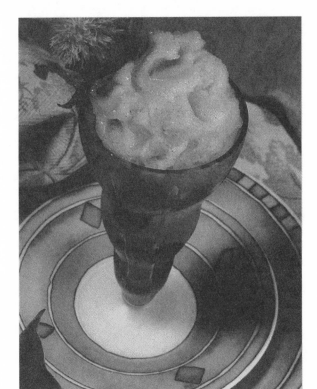

Michelle Huneven, a frequent contributor to The Times Food section, developed this poetic pear sorbet, perfumed with cinnamon, vanilla bean and grated orange zest. It manages to taste like fall even as it's cooling you off on a hot afternoon.

PEAR SORBET

Makes 6 Servings

1 CUP SUGAR

2 CUPS WATER

ZEST AND JUICE FROM 1 ORANGE

1/2 TEASPOON CINNAMON

1/2 VANILLA BEAN

4 TO 5 MEDIUM-LARGE BARTLETT OR COMICE PEARS, PEELED, SEEDED AND CHOPPED TO MAKE 2 CUPS FRUIT

Place sugar, water, orange zest and juice, cinnamon and vanilla bean in saucepan and bring to boil over medium-high heat. Stir until sugar has dissolved. Add pears and cook until tender, about 4 minutes. Remove vanilla bean and set aside.

Cool pear mixture until it can be handled. Place in blender and blend until almost smooth. Scrape out seeds from inside vanilla bean and add to blender contents; discard pod. Blend until very smooth.

Chill, then process in ice cream maker according to manufacturer's instructions. Makes 1 quart.

Each serving:
180 calories; 1 mg sodium; 0 cholesterol; 0 fat; 46 grams carbohydrates; 1 gram protein; 0.81 gram fiber.

Sautéing is seductively quick. Braising takes more time, but has merits of its own. This is the technique where you fry the ingredients briefly and then stew them covered with a small amount of liquid. Once the ingredients begin to stew you can mostly leave the dish alone as it cooks. Above all, braising develops rich, deep flavors no amount of sautéing can. This recipe, developed by Times Test Kitchen cook Mayi Brady, is a relatively gentle braise, starting with butter and finishing in cream that develops the flavor of pears wonderfully.

Here is a classic winter salad, substantial and full of crunch: sweet pears, bitter endive, pungent cheese and buttery walnuts. It's just the thing for curling up in front of the fire. Jana Lieblich of the Times Test Kitchen also makes a late-summer version with peaches (peeled and pitted, of course).

PEARS BRAISED
IN CREAM

Makes 4 Servings

1 1/2 TABLESPOONS BUTTER

1 TABLESPOON GRANULATED SUGAR

1 TABLESPOON BROWN SUGAR, PACKED

4 FIRM PEARS, PEELED, CORED AND HALVED

3/4 CUP HEAVY WHIPPING CREAM

Rub bottom of 9x6-inch baking dish with 1 tablespoon butter. Sprinkle both sugars evenly over bottom of dish. Place pears, cut-side down, in dish and dot with remaining 1/2 tablespoon butter. Bake at 350 degrees 20 minutes. Pour cream into dish and tilt dish back and forth several times to mix with butter-sugar mixture. Bake until pears are tender when pierced with sharp knife, about 15 minutes. Serve warm.

Each serving:
312 calories; 62 mg sodium; 73 mg cholesterol; 22 grams fat; 32 grams carbohydrates; 2 grams protein; 2.33 grams fiber.

PEAR SALAD WITH
BLUE CHEESE AND
WALNUTS

Makes 6 Servings

6 PEARS

6 HEADS Belgian ENDIVE

1 CUP CRUMBLED BLUE CHEESE

1 CUP CHOPPED WALNUTS

1/3 CUP WALNUT OIL

2 TABLESPOONS ORANGE JUICE

2 TABLESPOONS WHITE WINE OR CHAMPAGNE VINEGAR

1/4 TEASPOON SALT

FRESHLY GROUND BLACK PEPPER

Wash pears and remove stems. Slice in half and remove seedy centers. Cut each half lengthwise into 1/4-inch-thick slices.

Slice each head of endive crosswise into 1/8-inch pieces, stopping 1/2 inch from root end. Discard root end.

Combine pears, endive, blue cheese and walnuts in bowl.

Whisk together walnut oil, orange juice, white wine vinegar, salt and pepper to taste. Pour over salad and toss gently. Serve immediately.

Each serving:
443 calories; 527 mg sodium; 17 mg cholesterol; 32 grams fat; 32 grams carbohydrates; 15 grams protein; 6.10 grams fiber.

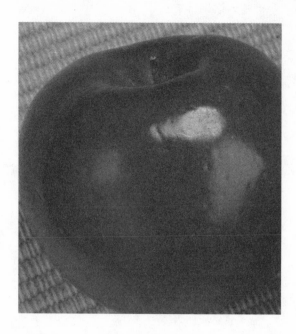

Apples

There are no fruits more romantically named than old-time apple varieties: Northern Spy, Stayman Winesap, Esopus Spitzenberg. Unfortunately, their romance is about all that's left. You'll probably never see them in the grocery store, except in a few isolated areas in the Midwest and Northeast.

Today's apple production is dominated by the West Coast, and very different varieties grow here—apples that don't need nearly as much cold weather.

The dominant apple varieties in the United States today are the Red and Golden Delicious, which were developed in Washington State. Granny Smith, which despite its homespun American name has its roots in Australia, follows. Japanese Fuji and New Zealand's Gala are right behind. Of these West Coast apples, the Granny Smith and the Fuji are the best for pies because their dense flesh will hold together during cooking.

ORIGINAL PANCAKE HOUSE APPLE PANCAKES

Makes 4 Pancakes or 8 Servings

8 EGGS

1 1/2 CUPS HALF AND HALF

DASH SALT

DASH NUTMEG

1 3/4 CUPS FLOUR

1/2 CUP POWDERED SUGAR

1/2 CUP BUTTER, CLARIFIED

2 POUNDS APPLES, PEELED AND THINLY SLICED

CINNAMON SUGAR

Combine eggs and half and half in large bowl and mix well. Add salt, nutmeg, flour and powdered sugar and mix until batter is smooth.

Heat 2 tablespoons butter in 7-inch oven-proof skillet over high heat and saute 1/2 pound apple slices until crisp-tender, about 5 minutes. Add 1 cup batter and bake at 425 degrees until firm, approximately 15 minutes.

Sprinkle top of pancake heavily with cinnamon sugar and slide pancake out onto plate. (Make cinnamon sugar by combining equal parts sugar and cinnamon.)

Invert pan over plate and turn, flipping pancake so second side is on top. Return to oven until done, about 5 more minutes. To serve, place plate upside-down on top of skillet and turn pan over, sliding pancake onto plate. Repeat with remaining batter.

Each serving:

680 calories; 230 mg sodium; 260 mg cholesterol; 23 grams fat; 100 grams carbohydrates; 18 grams protein; 0.77 gram fiber.

Former Times Wine Writer Dan Berger got this recipe from the Original Pancake House, a restaurant two hours from his Napa Valley home. He once talked his two young sons into getting up early enough to make the drive. When they arrived, they were shocked that he ordered just two pancakes for the party of four and dismayed at the prospect of a 20-minute wait while the pancakes baked. But after indulging in this breakfast treat, they agreed it was worth the drive and the wait. And that one of these pancakes is plenty for two people.

To clarify butter, heat it in a small saucepan over low heat until it melts and separates. Spoon off any foam on top. Then spoon off clear, clarified butter, leaving milky residue in pan.

Nothing is more American than apple pie. It's not that other nations don't make apple pie, or that we didn't get the idea from England, which probably got it from France in the first place. It's that apple pie is our universal vernacular dessert, made and loved everywhere. We Americans have made it our own with a more generous filling than is used in those flat little European fruit tarts and our own American flaky crust.

Here's another American idea for pie crust: adding cornmeal, for a warm hint of corn flavor and a bit of crunch. Cookbook author and Times columnist Marion Cunningham, who gave us this recipe, recommends Gravenstein apples.

CORNMEAL APPLE PIE

Makes 8 Servings

1 3/4 CUPS FLOUR

1/2 CUP YELLOW CORNMEAL

1/2 TEASPOON SALT

3/4 CUP SHORTENING

6 TO 8 TABLESPOONS WATER

8 LARGE APPLES, CORED, PEELED AND SLICED

1/2 TO 1 CUP SUGAR

1 TO 1 1/2 TEASPOONS CINNAMON

2 TABLESPOONS COLD BUTTER, CUT INTO SMALL DICE

Combine flour, cornmeal and salt in mixing bowl. Add shortening. Lightly rub shortening and flour together with hands or cut shortening and flour together with pastry blender until mixture resembles coarse meal. Slowly add water, stirring with fork until pastry holds together in rough ball.

Lightly flour board. Divide dough in half. Roll out half of dough into circle about 2 inches larger than 9-inch pie plate. Drape into bottom of pie plate.

Put apple slices in large bowl. Combine sugar and cinnamon in small bowl. Add to apple slices and stir gently to coat. Add more sugar to taste if needed.

Mound apple slices over dough in pie plate. Dot with butter. Roll remaining dough out to same size as bottom layer. Place over apples. Tuck edges under but above rim of pie plate. Crimp with fingers or use fork to finish edges.

Place pie on baking sheet to catch bubbling juices and bake at 450 degrees 15 minutes. Reduce heat to 350 degrees and continue baking until top is golden and juices are bubbling, 40 to 45 minutes. Serve warm.

Each serving:
464 calories; 178 mg sodium; 8 mg cholesterol; 23 grams fat; 64 grams carbohydrates; 4 grams protein; 0.82 gram fiber.

Mary Sue Milliken and Susan Feniger, famous to cable TV viewers across the country as the Too Hot Tamales, have operated a series of restaurants in Los Angeles. Their current restaurant is Border Grill in Santa Monica. Milliken's mother created this pie recipe for their second, City Restaurant. It combines good old apple pie with the insistent tanginess of cranberries. So here it is— Mom's apple-cranberry pie.

CITY RESTAURANT APPLE-CRANBERRY PIE

Makes 8 Servings

FILLING

5 EXTRA-LARGE GRANNY SMITH APPLES OR EQUIVALENT

1 (12-OUNCE) PACKAGE CRANBERRIES

1 1/2 CUPS SUGAR

1/4 CUP INSTANT TAPIOCA

PARTIALLY BAKED PIE SHELL

2 CUPS FLOUR

1/2 CUP LARD

1/4 CUP BUTTER

1 TEASPOON SALT

ICE WATER

STREUSEL

2/3 CUP BUTTER

3/4 CUP LIGHT BROWN SUGAR, PACKED

1/2 TEASPOON SALT

1 TEASPOON CINNAMON

1 1/2 CUPS FLOUR

FILLING

Peel, core and chop apples into pieces the size of cranberries. Place cranberries in food processor and chop briefly, about 10 seconds.

Combine apples and cranberries in large bowl. Add sugar and stir until fruit is coated. Cover bowl and set aside until juices from fruit flow freely and sugar is almost completely dissolved, 15 to 20 minutes.

Stir tapioca into fruit and juice. Let sit additional 10 to 15 minutes.

PARTIALLY BAKED PIE SHELL

Combine flour, lard, butter and salt in large bowl. Lightly work dough with fingertips until pieces of butter and lard are no larger than small peas. Add 1/3 cup ice water teaspoon by teaspoon, tossing flour mixture lightly with fork. If mixture seems too dry to press into ball, add up to another 1 tablespoon ice water.

Press mixture into ball. Wrap in plastic wrap. Let stand about 30 minutes in refrigerator. Roll to 1/8-inch thickness. Fit into 10-inch pie plate. Flute edge. Let stand again in refrigerator 30 minutes. Line shell with sheet of foil filled with pastry weights or uncooked navy beans.

Bake at 425 degrees until edges are light brown, 8 to 10 minutes. Remove foil and weights. Return to oven until bottom crust is set and no longer raw, about 2 minutes.

STREUSEL

Combine butter, brown sugar, salt, cinnamon and flour. Lightly work mixture with fingertips until butter is completely incorporated and mixture is crumbly.

ASSEMBLY

Fill Partially Baked Pie Shell with Filling. Sprinkle top generously with Streusel. Reserve any remaining Streusel for another use.

Bake at 325 degrees until filling bubbles in center, about 45 minutes. If edges of pie shell begin to brown too quickly, cover with strips of foil.

Each serving:
787 calories; 453 mg sodium; 68 mg cholesterol; 35 grams fat; 117 grams carbohydrates; 6 grams protein; 1.1 grams fiber.

Persimmons are regularly used in baked dishes such as persimmon bread. But in California, persimmon season weather can be ovenlike. Make your persimmons into ice cream and you get all the same spicy flavor without making your kitchen uninhabitably hot. This recipe comes from frequent Times Food Section contributor Michelle Huneven.

The ripeness of the persimmons is everything in this dish. They should be completely soft, maybe with some black spots on the skin. Really ripe persimmons make almost any addition seem beside the point. Sugar? They couldn't be any sweeter. Spice? They are profoundly scented with what seems like cloves, cinnamon and ginger. The recipe is from Times Staff Writer Russ Parsons.

PERSIMMON ICE CREAM

Makes 6 Servings

4 TO 6 RIPE PERSIMMONS	PINCH CLOVES
1/2 TEASPOON CINNAMON	PINCH MACE, OPTIONAL
1/4 TEASPOON GINGER OR 1/2 TEASPOON GRATED GINGER ROOT	3/4 CUP SUGAR
	2 CUPS HALF AND HALF
PINCH ALLSPICE	

Peel, seed and coarsely chop persimmons to yield about 2 cups. Press persimmons through ricer or pulse few times in blender. Place in bowl. Add cinnamon, ginger, allspice, cloves and mace. Stir together, then chill in refrigerator.

Add sugar and stir until dissolved, about 3 minutes. Combine persimmon mixture and half and half in ice cream maker and process according to manufacturer's instructions until set. Makes 1 quart.

Each serving:
314 calories; 32 mg sodium; 69 mg cholesterol; 19 grams fat; 35 grams carbohydrates; 2 grams protein; 0.32 gram fiber.

PERSIMMON PARFAIT

Makes 4 Servings

1 CUP WALNUT PIECES	1 TABLESPOON SUGAR
4 PERSIMMONS	2 TEASPOONS WHISKEY OR BOURBON
1/2 CUP WHIPPING CREAM	

Toast walnut pieces in dry skillet over medium heat just until fragrant. Chop coarsely.

Set persimmons on tops, with pointed end up. Divide in quarters without cutting completely through. Place each persimmon in bowl.

Whip cream to soft peaks. Add sugar and beat until bit of cream rubbed between fingers no longer feels gritty. Beat in whiskey.

Open persimmon quarters like flower. Spoon dollop of whipped cream in center. Sprinkle with chopped walnuts.

Each serving:
345 calories; 15 mg sodium; 41 mg cholesterol; 30 grams fat; 18 grams carbohydrates; 5 grams protein; 1.75 grams fiber.

Here is a fruit stew—a compote by any other name. You can vary the fruit in it, depending on what is available. The sauce is a little tart, and the fruit is a little sweet. Frequent Times Food section contributor Michelle Huneven created the stew, which is perfect over ice cream or with a dollop of vanilla yogurt. Ginger snaps or molasses crinkles are the perfect accompaniment.

FALL FRUIT STEW

Makes 6 Servings

2 CUPS UNSWEETENED APPLE JUICE	**4 PLUMS, PITTED, CUT IN HALVES**
1 CUP WATER	**2 FUYU PERSIMMONS, PEELED, SEEDED, CUT IN EIGHTHS**
2 CINNAMON STICKS	**1/3 CUP GOLDEN RAISINS**
1 (1-INCH) PIECE GINGER ROOT, CUT IN HALF	**1/3 CUP DARK RAISINS**
ZEST OF 1 ORANGE	**1/2 CUP PITTED PRUNES**
ZEST OF 1 LEMON	**1/2 CUP DRIED APRICOTS**
2 APPLES, PEELED, CORED, CUT IN EIGHTHS	**1/3 CUP FRESH RASPBERRIES**
2 FIRM PEARS, PEELED, CORED, CUT IN EIGHTHS	**1/4 CUP ALMONDS, CHOPPED**
	POMEGRANATE SEEDS

Bring apple juice, water, cinnamon sticks, ginger and orange and lemon zests to boil in large saucepan. Add apples, cover and cook until just tender, about 15 minutes. Add pears, cover, and cook 5 minutes. Add plums, persimmons, golden and dark raisins, prunes and apricots and cook another 5 minutes. If you must stir, be careful not to break fruit apart. Turn off heat. Gently stir in raspberries.

Toast almonds in 400-degree oven until golden brown, about 3 minutes.

Remove ginger root and carefully spoon stew into individual bowls, being careful not to break up fruit. Serve stew sprinkled with toasted almonds and pomegranate seeds.

Each serving:
277 calories; 7 mg sodium; 0 cholesterol; 4 grams fat; 65 grams carbohydrates; 3 grams protein; 2.88 grams fiber.

Winter is a time for

a tangerine dream

fennel gratin

caramelized carrots

a sauté of chanterelle mushrooms

grapefruit slices, pink and yellow

good-luck oranges

stalks of broccoli

heads of escarole

garlicky baked cauliflower

puckery pickled lemons

fresh-squeezed blood-orange juice

the heady scent of citrus trees,

perfuming the season with promises of spring to come.

winter

Times Restaurant Critic S. Irene Virbila learned this simple, elegant recipe from Cesare Giaccone, who has become world-famous while working in an impossibly tiny restaurant named Ristorante Cacciatori (but known to everybody as "da Cesare") in the Barolo country of the Piedmont. Giaccone specializes in exquisite traditional dishes, often with an imaginative twist, always using the best local ingredients.

CORNMEAL PASTA WITH LEEKS

Makes 4 Servings

LEEK SAUCE

1/4 CUP BUTTER

1 POUND SLENDER LEEKS, WHITE PART ONLY, FINELY SLICED

1/2 CUP WHIPPING CREAM

2/3 CUP OR MORE RICH HOMEMADE BROTH

SALT, PEPPER

CORNMEAL PASTA

1 CUP FINELY GROUND CORNMEAL

1 1/2 CUPS FLOUR

PINCH SALT

5 EGGS

1 TABLESPOON OLIVE OIL

LEEK SAUCE

Heat butter in skillet over medium heat and gently stew leeks until slightly brown, about 15 minutes. Add cream, then broth. Cook over medium heat until sauce is bubbling, about 10 minutes. Season to taste with salt and pepper.

CORNMEAL PASTA

Mix cornmeal, flour and salt and mound on work surface. Make well in center. Break eggs into well and add oil. Beat eggs with fork, gradually incorporating flour from sides of well. Scrape up any scraps and knead into dough. Knead in more flour if needed to make workable soft dough. Flour work surface and knead dough until smooth and elastic and no longer sticky, 10 to 12 minutes.

Divide dough into 4 roughly equal lumps. Flatten 1 lump on lightly floured surface and roll out 1/8 inch thick with rolling pin. (Cornmeal dough is easy to work but too soft for pasta machine.) Repeat with remaining dough.

Lay out pasta sheets on work table or wooden surface to dry. When pasta is no longer tacky, roll up each strip and cut by hand into 1/2- to 3/4-inch noodles.

Cook Cornmeal Pasta in boiling, lightly salted water until al dente, about 5 minutes. Top each serving with Leek Sauce.

Each serving:
604 calories; 599 mg sodium; 263 mg cholesterol; 34 grams fat; 60 grams carbohydrates; 15 grams protein; 2.23 grams fiber.

BRAISED DUCK
AND LENTILS

Makes 6 Servings

4 CARROTS	6 DUCK LEGS (ABOUT 3 POUNDS)
2 ONIONS	4 PLUM TOMATOES
2 STALKS CELERY	3 SLICES PROSCIUTTO
2 CLOVES GARLIC	2 SHALLOTS
1 (750-ML) BOTTLE RED WINE	2 TABLESPOONS BUTTER
2 TABLESPOONS RED WINE VINEGAR	1 TABLESPOON OIL
2 WHOLE CLOVES	SALT, PEPPER
1/4 TEASPOON BLACK PEPPERCORNS	1 POUND LENTILS
	MINCED PARSLEY

Chop 2 carrots, 1 onion, 1 stalk celery and garlic.

Bring wine, vinegar, chopped carrots, onion, celery and garlic as well as cloves and peppercorns to boil in 2-quart saucepan over medium heat. Remove from heat and cool slightly.

Place duck legs in 1 layer in large baking dish and pour wine mixture over. Cover tightly and marinate, refrigerated, overnight.

Next day, peel, seed and chop tomatoes and mince prosciutto and shallots. Chop remaining carrots, onion and celery. Melt 1 tablespoon butter with prosciutto in heavy Dutch oven over medium-low heat. When prosciutto starts to cook, add carrots, onion, celery, shallots and tomatoes and cook, covered, until vegetables begin to soften, 10 to 15 minutes.

While vegetables are cooking, combine remaining 1 tablespoon butter and oil in large skillet over high heat. Remove duck legs from marinade, reserving marinade, and pat dry with paper towels. Sprinkle duck legs lightly with salt and pepper on both sides. When fat is very hot, add duck legs, skin side down, and brown well just on the skin side, 3 to 5 minutes. Remove duck legs from pan and set skin-side up atop vegetables in Dutch oven.

Pour off fat from skillet and strain marinade into skillet over high heat, scraping bottom to loosen any browned bits sticking to pan. Pour marinade over duck legs and vegetables. Place sheet of aluminum foil over, but not touching, duck legs and seal tightly. Bake at 300 degrees until duck legs are fork-tender, about 1 1/2 hours.

When duck legs are tender, remove from pan and set aside, covered.

Spoon off as much fat as possible. Add lentils to pan, cover, and cook until lentils are soft, about 40 minutes, adding another 1/2 cup water if necessary to keep lentils moist, but not soupy. When lentils are soft, add duck legs to pan, cover and cook just until heated through, 10 to 15 minutes. Sprinkle with minced parsley and serve.

Each serving:
753 calories; 249 mg sodium; 95 mg cholesterol; 50 grams fat; 41 grams carbohydrates; 31 grams protein; 3.68 grams fiber.

Dealing with duck fat is the biggest technical challenge in this dish developed by Times Staff Writer Russ Parsons. There are two ways to go about it: You can simply remove the skin (which contains almost all of the fat) from the legs and then cook the legs by themselves. The problem is that you need some of the fat from the skin to keep the legs moist. A better solution, though it takes a little more effort, is to brown the legs on the skin side first (not on the meat side—that will toughen them up faster than anything), and then, before you add the lentils, skim the cooked stew of all fat. You have to be really rigorous about this. On one try, we skimmed more than 2 cups of fat before we quit counting.

You also could prepare the stew the night before and refrigerate it until the fat hardens. It can be spooned off quite easily at that point, though you'll probably end up losing some of the vegetables as well.

117

FENNEL GRATIN
(GRATIN DE FENOUIL)

Makes 6 to 8 Servings

BUTTER	SALT, PEPPER
1 CARROT, THINLY SLICED	1 SMALL ONION, MINCED
2 ONIONS, THINLY SLICED	1/4 CUP FLOUR
1 BAY LEAF	4 CUPS MILK
2 SPRIGS FRESH THYME, OR 1/2 TEASPOON DRIED	1/4 CUP WHIPPING CREAM
	1 EGG YOLK
4 LARGE BULBS FENNEL, 1 INCH OF BRANCHES ATTACHED	2 TABLESPOONS GRATED GRUYERE CHEESE

Melt 2 tablespoons butter in bottom of oven-proof casserole or Dutch oven big enough to hold 4 whole fennel bulbs. Add carrot, sliced onions, bay leaf and thyme, and cook until just softened, about 5 minutes.

Place whole fennel bulbs on top of vegetables, season with salt and pepper to taste and add water to cover. Butter sheet of aluminum foil and place over fennel bulbs. Cover with heat-proof plate to keep fennel submerged and then cover tightly. Bake at 400 degrees until fennel is tender enough to pierce easily with knife, about 1 hour. Be careful not to overcook; fennel must not be soft or mushy.

While fennel is cooking, cook minced small onion over low heat in 1 tablespoon butter until very soft, 15 to 20 minutes. Do not let brown.

Melt 1/4 cup butter in medium saucepan over medium heat. Add flour and stir to combine. Cook 2 to 3 minutes, then add cold milk. Cook, stirring with whisk, until mixture thickens, about 10 minutes. Add minced onion and whipping cream and cook over low heat at least 20 minutes.

When sauce is thick and creamy and has lost any taste of raw flour, remove from heat and divide into 2 bowls and set aside. When slightly cooled, beat egg yolk into sauce in 1 bowl until completely mixed. (Dish can be made to this point 1 day ahead and fennel bulbs refrigerated in cooking liquid.)

Remove fennel from cooking liquid and set aside until cool enough to handle. Trim away branches and cut bulbs lengthwise in 1/2-inch slices.

Heat nonstick skillet over medium-high heat. When very hot, add 1/2 tablespoon butter. When butter is sizzling, add half of fennel slices and cook until brown, 2 to 3 minutes. Carefully turn over and brown on second side, another 2 minutes.

When first batch is finished, place in single overlapping layer in large buttered gratin dish. Spoon over cream sauce without egg. Fry remaining fennel in same way and place in gratin dish in single overlapping layer. Spoon over cream sauce with egg and smooth sauce to cover.

Bake at 400 degrees until puffy in center and browned on edges, about 45 minutes. (Dish can be made ahead to this point several hours in advance and refrigerated.)

Just before serving, sprinkle gratin with cheese and broil until cheese melts and crust forms, 2 to 3 minutes. If dish has been refrigerated, bring to room temperature 30 to 40 minutes before sprinkling with cheese and broiling.

Each of 8 servings:
178 calories; 175 mg sodium; 66 mg cholesterol; 11 grams fat; 16 grams carbohydrates; 6 grams protein; 0.30 gram fiber.

Summer is the greens season, but winter brings its own range of choices. This recipe by cookbook author and Times columnist Marion Cunningham highlights the mildly spicy flavor of mustard greens; collard, turnip or dandelion greens could be substituted.

If you happen to have leftover cooked turnips and navy beans, the soup is ready in less than half an hour. If you don't, diced turnips only take 15 to 20 minutes to cook. Beans take longer. Rinse the beans and pick them over carefully to remove stones and withered and broken beans. Bring them to a boil (allowing 1 quart water to 1 pound beans) and boil 2 minutes, then cover and remove from the fire and let stand 1 hour. Simmer the beans until tender, 1 to 1 1/2 hours.

MUSTARD GREEN SOUP

Makes 4 Servings

3/4 POUND (ABOUT 6 CUPS) MUSTARD GREENS	2 CUPS COOKED, DICED TURNIPS
1/4 CUP OLIVE OIL	2 CUPS COOKED NAVY BEANS
1 TABLESPOON FINELY CHOPPED GARLIC	8 CUPS CHICKEN OR VEGETABLE BROTH
1 CUP CHOPPED ONIONS	SALT, PEPPER

Wash greens well. Trim tough stems. Chop and set aside.

Heat olive oil in soup kettle or pot. Add garlic and onions and cook over medium-low heat, stirring often, until garlic and onions are softened but not browned, about 5 minutes. Stir in turnips, beans, greens and broth. Season to taste with salt and pepper. Simmer about 15 minutes. Serve hot.

Each serving:
381 calories; 1,689 mg sodium; 2 mg cholesterol; 17 grams fat; 38 grams carbohydrates; 21 grams protein; 4.62 grams fiber.

PORK AND BEANS
. . . AND ENDIVE

Makes 8 to 10 Servings

2 TABLESPOONS OLIVE OIL

1 POUND ITALIAN SAUSAGE

1 1/2 POUNDS COUNTRY-STYLE PORK RIBS

SALT, PEPPER

2 CARROTS, CHOPPED

2 ONIONS, CHOPPED

3 CLOVES GARLIC, SLICED

1 POUND DRIED BEANS

WATER

2 CUPS CHOPPED CURLY ENDIVE, TOUGH GREEN LEAVES ONLY

Heat oil in heavy Dutch oven over medium-high heat. Cut sausages in half. Sprinkle ribs with salt and pepper to taste. Brown sausages and ribs in hot oil. Remove to plate and set aside.

Pour off all but 2 tablespoons fat and add carrots, onions and garlic to pan. Reduce heat to medium, cover and cook, stirring occasionally, until vegetables soften, 3 to 5 minutes. Scrape bottom of pan while stirring to free brown bits.

Place beans in pan and stir to mix with vegetables. Add 5 cups water and 2 teaspoons salt and return meat to pan. Cover and bake at 300 degrees until beans soften, 2 to 2 1/2 hours. After first hour, check beans every 30 minutes, stirring and adding more water if necessary. Dish should have stew-like texture when beans are done.

When beans have softened, remove from oven and add chopped endive. Stir well to mix and set aside until endive has wilted, 5 to 10 minutes.

Each of 8 servings:
557 calories; 547 mg sodium; 78 mg cholesterol; 33 grams fat; 38 grams carbohydrates; 27 grams protein; 3.58 grams fiber.

Take pork and beans, replace the side bacon with country-style ribs and Italian sausage, throw in some garlic, olive oil and endive, and hold the molasses. Ecco: a distinctly different dish, developed by Times Staff Writer Russ Parsons. Those who disdain the idea of matching food and wine, he suggests, should try this dish with any old red wine and then with a decent Chianti; it's an absolutely superb match.

Cookbook author and Times columnist Marion Cunningham calls this one of her old standbys, a comforting dish in which virtually nothing can go wrong. The dish keeps well, too; double the recipe and enjoy it again another day.

SCALLOPED GARLIC POTATOES

Makes 4 to 6 Servings

5 BAKING POTATOES, PEELED AND SLICED

BUTTER

SALT

4 LARGE CLOVES GARLIC, FINELY CHOPPED

1 1/2 CUPS MILK

1/3 CUP WHIPPING CREAM

Place potatoes in 1 layer in bottom of buttered 8-inch-square baking dish. Salt lightly and sprinkle with garlic. Repeat in layers until all potatoes are used. Pour milk evenly over potatoes.

Bake uncovered at 325 degrees 45 minutes. Remove from oven and drizzle cream over potatoes. Return to oven and bake 45 minutes. Serve hot. If not serving right away, cool potatoes, cover tightly with foil and freeze until needed.

Each of 6 servings:
152 calories; 91 mg sodium; 23 mg cholesterol; 6 grams fat; 21 grams carbohydrates; 4 grams protein; 0.44 gram fiber.

SAVORY BAKED SWEET POTATOES

Makes 4 Servings

4 SWEET POTATOES, ABOUT 3/4 POUND EACH

FRESH ROSEMARY SPRIGS

2 TO 4 LARGE CLOVES GARLIC, PEELED, THINLY SLICED

NONSTICK COOKING SPRAY

SALT

CRACKED BLACK PEPPER

Clean sweet potatoes under running water and pat dry. Make deep crosswise cuts about every inch, 2 to 3 cuts per potato; cut almost but not quite through, leaving potatoes intact. Insert several sprigs rosemary and few slices garlic deep into cuts.

Place on baking sheet and spray potatoes with cooking spray. Season with salt and pepper to taste. Bake at 375 degrees just until potatoes are tender and lightly browned, about 1 hour.

Each serving:
319 calories; 98 mg sodium; 0 cholesterol; 0 fat; 75 grams carbohydrates; 4 grams protein; 2.71 grams fiber.

When it comes to sweet potatoes, most cooks emphasize the "sweet" and overlook the "potato." But this nutritious vegetable doesn't have to be baked in the usual buttery brown-sugar glaze. It's excellent prepared as an Italian cook might treat white potatoes, fragrant with garlic and rosemary. This recipe by Times Test Kitchen Director Donna Deane reduces the calories even more by using low-fat cooking spray instead of oil. Select sweet potatoes that are about the same size. They should be the sweet, moist, dark-skinned type with orange flesh, not the pale, yellowish variety. The potatoes are sliced deeply and baked with the garlic and rosemary in the cuts. After about an hour, the potatoes and the tips of the rosemary sprigs will be browned and full of flavor.

It's an ever-grow-ing challenge—what to serve when your guests are a mixture of vegetar-ians and meat-eaters. Vegetarians may be willing to sacrifice many pleasures for their diet, but it's unfair to demand the same of everyone else. One happy solution is veg-etable lasagna. It seems to work where other pasta dishes don't, possi-bly because all that cheese makes it feel more substantial.

BROCCOLI LASAGNA

Makes 6 to 8 Servings

LASAGNA NOODLES

Flour

1/2 TEASPOON SALT

1 TABLESPOON OLIVE OIL

2 EGGS

WATER

SPICY TOMATO SAUCE

2 TABLESPOONS OLIVE OIL

1 ONION, MINCED

4 CLOVES GARLIC, MINCED

1 (28-OUNCE) CAN TOMATOES

1 TEASPOON RED PEPPER FLAKES

SALT, PEPPER

BROCCOLI FILLING

1 POUND BROCCOLI

1/2 POUND BROCCOLI RABE

SALT

1 (15-OUNCE) PACKAGE RICOTTA

1/2 POUND FRESH GOAT CHEESE

1 TABLESPOON GRATED PECORINO ROMANO

ASSEMBLY

1 TABLESPOON MINCED PARSLEY

LASAGNA NOODLES

Combine 1 1/2 cups flour, salt and olive oil in bowl of food processor fitted with steel blade. Pulse once or twice to combine. Add eggs and process until dough forms rough ball that holds together, about 20 seconds. If necessary, slowly add up to 1 tablespoon water. Continue processing 10 to 15 seconds to knead. Wrap dough tightly in plastic wrap and set aside to rest for 30 minutes.

Cut dough in half; cover half with damp tea towel. Flatten remaining half by hand, then dust lightly with flour and pass through widest setting on pasta machine. Fold double, dust and roll again. Repeat until dough becomes silky to touch, 7 or 8 passes.

When dough is correct texture, roll out in pasta machine in ever-narrowing widths as thin as you can without tearing noodles. Hang noodles to dry and repeat with remaining dough.

SPICY TOMATO SAUCE

Heat oil in medium saucepan and add onion and garlic and cook over medium-low heat until translucent, about 10 minutes. Add tomatoes and red pepper flakes and cook until tomatoes begin to fall apart, about 5 minutes.

Purée sauce through food mill into another saucepan. Cook sauce over medium heat until smooth and combined, about 10 minutes. Season to taste with salt and pepper.

BROCCOLI FILLING

Separate and reserve florets from broccoli stalks. Peel broccoli stalks, trim ends and cut in small cubes. Separate and reserve leaves from broccoli rabe and cut stems in small cubes.

Cook broccoli and broccoli rabe stems in plenty of rapidly boiling, salted water until tender-crisp, 5 to 7 minutes. Remove from water and drain. Add reserved florets and leaves to boiling water and cook until tender, 2 to 3 minutes. Remove and drain. Chop leaves and florets in rough pieces.

Combine broccoli and broccoli rabe stems, leaves and florets, ricotta, goat cheese and Romano cheese in bowl. Mix well and add salt to taste. Romano is salty, so be cautious.

ASSEMBLY

Cook lasagna noodles 2 pieces at a time in plenty of rapidly boiling salted water. Noodles will float to top of water when cooked, about 1 to 2 minutes.

Spread 1/2 cup Spicy Tomato Sauce in bottom of lightly oiled 13x9-inch glass baking dish. Place 1 layer Lasagna Noodles over sauce. Top with 1/4 Broccoli Filling and spread evenly over noodles. Repeat, alternating noodles and filling until all filling is used, ending with layer of noodles. Compress and smooth filling by pressing lightly on top layer with palm of hand.

Spread remaining Spicy Tomato Sauce over top of lasagna and bake at 350 degrees until heated through, about 20 to 30 minutes. Before serving, sprinkle with minced parsley.

Each of 6 servings:
485 calories; 776 mg sodium; 125 mg cholesterol; 27 grams fat; 38 grams carbohydrates; 25 grams protein; 2.14 grams fiber.

Times Staff Writer Russ Parsons' version of vegetable lasagna is filled with a mixture of broccoli and broccoli rabe. The latter—a relative of broccoli popular in Italy, where it is known as rapini—*has been catching on in this country. It has a spicy taste with a slightly bitter edge that makes it a nice counterpoint to the richness of the cheese. But if you can't find broccoli rabe, use 1 1/2 pounds of broccoli.*

Fresh pasta makes a huge difference in lasagna. Instead of being a bookmark dividing the layers, a fresh noodle is the light, silky soul of the dish.

The slightly bitter flavor of escarole and the tartness of lemon juice give the chicken broth in this soup a light, clean taste. Times Test Kitchen Director Donna Deane created the soup as an antidote to the annual glut of holiday buffets, cookie plates and endless food gifts.

You get more flavor when you poach the chicken in nonfat chicken broth instead of water. Be sure to skim excess fat off the broth before adding the escarole. A large soup plate of this is substantial enough for a meal. Note that the fat count can be lowered significantly through diligent skimming. These figures reflect standard skimming.

ESCAROLE CHICKEN SOUP

Makes 6 to 8 Servings

1 (1 1/2- TO 2-POUND) CHICKEN

2 (49 1/2-OUNCE) CANS NONFAT CHICKEN BROTH

1 CELERY TOP

1 SMALL ONION, QUARTERED

NONSTICK COOKING SPRAY

3 CLOVES GARLIC, MINCED

1 HEAD ESCAROLE, CUT INTO 1-INCH CROSSWISE SLICES

2 TABLESPOONS LEMON JUICE

LIME SLICES

SPRIGS OF CILANTRO

Wash chicken well and remove giblets. Save liver for another use and set aside remaining giblets.

Place whole chicken in soup pot along with chicken broth, celery top and onion. Add reserved giblets. Bring to boil. Reduce heat, cover and simmer until chicken is tender, 35 to 45 minutes. Remove chicken from broth and let cool. Refrigerate chicken broth and chicken overnight or let broth stand until fat rises to top. Skim off excess fat and strain. Remove skin from chicken and discard. Cover meat and set aside.

Lightly spray wok or skillet with nonstick cooking spray. Add garlic and sauté lightly. Add escarole and cook, stirring, until tender, about 10 minutes. Add escarole to broth and heat to boiling. Stir in lemon juice.

Slice chicken breast and arrange several slices in bottom of large soup plates. Spoon broth over top. Garnish each with lime slice and cilantro sprig.

Each of 8 servings:
137 calories; 136 mg sodium; 33 mg cholesterol; 8 grams fat; 4 grams carbohydrates; 12 grams protein; 0.17 gram fiber.

Like most nuts, walnuts develop a richer flavor when toasted. Only then can they really stand up to the robust flavor of blue cheese. Walnuts and cheese add richness to this celery salad; the celery's contribution is, of course, juiciness, crunch and sharp, herby aroma. Times Staff Writer Russ Parsons advises slicing the celery about 1/4 inch thick. That way, he says, the celery holds its own (when celery is sliced thinner, it becomes a background flavor) and you get an even distribution of flavors in every bite.

CELERY SALAD WITH WALNUTS AND BLUE CHEESE

Makes 6 Servings

3/4 TEASPOON MINCED SHALLOTS

1 TABLESPOON SHERRY VINEGAR

3/4 CUP WALNUTS

1 BUNCH CELERY, BOTTOMS AND LEAFY TOPS TRIMMED

1/4 CUP OLIVE OIL

1 CUP CRUMBLED BLUE CHEESE

SALT

FRESHLY GROUND PEPPER

Combine shallots and vinegar in small bowl and set aside.

Toast walnuts on baking sheet in 350-degree oven or over medium heat in small skillet. When walnuts become fragrant, remove from heat. Do not scorch walnuts. Set aside.

Slice celery about 1/4 inch thick, cutting on bias to make exaggerated V-shaped pieces. Place in large serving bowl.

Add oil to shallots and vinegar and whisk to combine. (Do not season at this time; many blue cheeses are very salty.)

Coarsely chop walnuts and add to celery. Pour half to two-thirds of dressing over salad and toss to coat well. Add more dressing as needed; salad should be moistened, but there shouldn't be leftover dressing in bottom of bowl. Add blue cheese and toss lightly to combine. Taste and add salt, if needed, and pepper to taste.

Each serving:
269 calories; 434 mg sodium; 17 mg cholesterol; 25 grams fat; 6 grams carbohydrates; 8 grams protein; 1.33 grams fiber.

Lemons

Lemons are part rind, part juice, part magic.
—Sylvia Thompson

A lemon tree, especially a Meyer lemon tree, can bear so heavily that the lucky cook will have more lemons than he or she can use for all but two or three months of the year. Lemons are in their prime, however, during the winter months. A Meyer lemon is somewhat sweeter than a normal lemon, with an almost tangerine-like complexity—sometimes there's even a note of lavender— and it has a thinner, more fragrant rind. For this reason, it is a favorite of discerning home cooks.

How to Pickle Lemons (or Limes)

Everybody knows that lemons symbolize freshness. Cooks know it. Detergent manufacturers certainly know it. But there's another kind of lemon flavor without that sharp, clean pungency—a mellow sort of lemoniness, plush, perfumed and exotic. In English it goes by names like salted or pickled lemons. The Moroccans use a more poetic expression: *lim mraqqed*, "lemons that have been put to sleep."

They perfume many Moroccan dishes, but there's no need to limit them to traditional uses. Mince some into salad for a whiff of mystery. Add them to scrambled eggs, curry or lobster salad. Along with a little garlic and cilantro, mix them with roasted peppers or lightly toasted chopped walnut meats for an exotic relish. Add some of the pickling juice to a vinaigrette. Don't overdo it, though—the aroma is so heavy that it can cloy.

By the way, this is one recipe you *shouldn't* use Meyer lemons for. The flavor does not improve.

Step 1—Wash and scrub the lemons or limes; there's often a thin layer of wax or other preservative on the peel. Cut each fruit nearly into four pieces by making two cuts at right angles to each other from one end of the fruit almost to the other, leaving enough uncut that fruit can be opened without falling apart, about 1/2 inch.

Step 2: Generously salt the exposed flesh, using at least 3 tablespoons per pound of lemons.

Step 3: Put the salted fruits in a big, scrupulously clean jar and cover with fresh lemon juice or water. Lemon juice gives a better flavor, but resist the temptation to use bottled lemon juice, which gives an unpleasant metallic quality. Put on the lid and leave the jar at room temperature for four or five weeks.

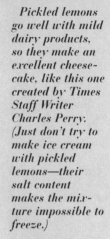

Pickled lemons go well with mild dairy products, so they make an excellent cheesecake, like this one created by Times Staff Writer Charles Perry. (Just don't try to make ice cream with pickled lemons—their salt content makes the mixture impossible to freeze.)

Three pickled limes may be substituted for the two pickled lemons to get a slightly different flavor.

PICKLED LEMON CHEESECAKE

Makes 8 Servings

CHEESECAKE

1 POUND RICOTTA CHEESE

1 CUP SUGAR

3 EGGS

2 PICKLED LEMONS, SEEDED AND DICED PLUS EXTRA SLICES FOR GARNISH

3 TABLESPOONS FLOUR

PASTA FROLLA

3/4 CUP FLOUR

3 TABLESPOONS SUGAR

3 TABLESPOONS BUTTER, AT ROOM TEMPERATURE

1 EGG

CHEESECAKE

Combine ricotta, sugar and eggs in mixing bowl. Add diced pickled lemons. Stir in flour and mix well. Set aside until ready to fill Pasta Frolla.

PASTA FROLLA

Combine flour and sugar in mixing bowl. Cut butter into flour mixture until crumbly. Mix with egg.

Knead just until mixture can be formed into ball. Cover with plastic wrap. Let stand 30 minutes at room temperature.

Roll out and line 8-inch springform pan with dough. Pour in Cheesecake mixture. Bake at 375 degrees 40 minutes. Remove from oven. Let stand 30 minutes before slicing or removing from pan. When cool, refrigerate. Garnish, if wished, with thin slices of pickled lemon.

Each serving:
457 calories; 166 mg sodium; 195 mg cholesterol; 19 grams fat; 60 grams carbohydrates; 15 grams protein; 0.05 gram fiber.

Ah, winter; 'tis the season to overeat. If you've made a New Year's resolution to cut down on calories—or if you just want a break from those heavy holiday foods—this refreshing ice from Times Test Kitchen Director Donna Deane can help. It not only tastes great but also has a beautiful pink hue. The amount of sugar will vary according to the sweetness of the grapefruit; some people love it without any sugar at all. The ice is best when served slightly slushy.

The Meyer lemon, less tart and more richly aromatic than the usual lemon, is actually a cross between a lemon and an orange, which makes it a natural candidate for marmalade. You can often find Meyers in markets during the winter. Substitute regular lemons in this recipe by Times Staff Writer Russ Parsons if you want, but you'll be missing out on the Meyer's unique flavor.

GRAPEFRUIT ICE

Makes 4 Servings

2 CUPS PINK GRAPEFRUIT JUICE (ABOUT 3 GRAPEFRUIT)

1/4 CUP SUGAR

1 TABLESPOON GRAND MARNIER

1 TABLESPOON LIME JUICE

Combine grapefruit juice, sugar, Grand Marnier and lime juice. Freeze in ice cream maker according to manufacturer's instructions. Spoon into chilled glass dishes, cover and freeze until serving time.

Each serving:
105 calories; 1 mg sodium; 0 cholesterol; 0 fat; 24 grams carbohydrates; 1 gram protein; 0 fiber.

MEYER LEMON MARMALADE

Makes 3 (1/2-pint) Jars

4 TO 5 MEYER LEMONS, ABOUT 1 1/4 POUNDS

2 1/2 TO 3 CUPS WATER

3 1/3 CUPS SUGAR

Thinly slice lemons and discard ends and seeds. Place lemon slices in large bowl and barely cover with water. Let stand overnight.

Place lemons and soaking water in large non-reactive preserving pan. Add sugar (2/3 cup sugar for every 1 cup lemon-water). Bring to boil. When foam begins to build, after 15 to 20 minutes, reduce heat just low enough to keep mixture from boiling over. Cook until jelly thermometer reaches 220 degrees.

Ladle into sterilized jars and attach clean lids. Lower jars into boiling water to cover and boil 5 minutes. Remove and cool. When cool, press lightly on top of lid; it should not pop back. If lid pops back, repeat heating process.

Each 1-tablespoon serving:
56 calories; 0 sodium; 0 cholesterol; 0 fat; 15 grams carbohydrates; 0 protein; 0 fiber.

In Southern California, oranges in winter are as abundant as zucchini in August. If you have an orange tree, you can never have too many orange recipes. Fortunately, oranges make an excellent flavoring for crème brûlée, that crusty custard familiar from a thousand restaurant dessert lists. This recipe from "Williams-Sonoma: Festive Occasions Cook" by Joyce Goldstein and Chuck Williams (Weldon Owen, 1993) calls for a mixture of oranges and blood oranges, a variety with a startlingly dark red-orange juice. If you can't find blood oranges, you can substitute regular oranges, though at the loss of a truly dramatic color.

BLOOD-ORANGE CRÈME BRÛLÉE

Makes 20 Servings

1 3/4 CUPS ORANGE JUICE

1/4 CUP BLOOD ORANGE JUICE OR REGULAR ORANGE JUICE

1 CUP ORANGE-FLAVORED LIQUEUR

4 CUPS WHIPPING CREAM

GRATED ZEST OF 4 BLOOD ORANGES OR REGULAR ORANGES

1 1/2 CUPS GRANULATED SUGAR

14 EGG YOLKS

1/4 CUP BROWN SUGAR, PACKED

Cook orange juice, blood orange juice and orange-flavored liqueur in small saucepan over high heat until reduced to 1 cup, about 15 minutes. Set aside.

Cook cream, blood orange zest and granulated sugar in separate saucepan, stirring, until sugar is dissolved, about 5 minutes. Remove from heat, cover and let steep at least 45 minutes.

Beat egg yolks until light. Strain cream mixture into yolks, stirring with whisk to combine. Stir in juice mixture. Pour into 13x9-inch baking dish. Place baking dish in slightly larger baking pan and add hot water to halfway up sides of baking dish. Bake at 350 degrees until just set, about 1 hour. Remove from baking pan and refrigerate.

When cool, cover and chill thoroughly. To serve, sprinkle brown sugar over custard. Place in baking pan and broil until sugar caramelizes, 3 to 4 minutes. Alternatively, heat brown sugar topping with propane torch until melted. Set aside until sugar hardens, about 1 minute.

Serve by scooping out of baking dish into individual dessert dishes.

Each serving:
311 calories; 25 mg sodium; 257 mg cholesterol; 22 grams fat; 21 grams carbohydrates; 3 grams protein; 0.03 gram fiber.

When Times Staff Writer Russ Parsons got a waffle maker, he found himself on a quest for the Perfect Waffle. He added sour cream and buttermilk to the usual recipe to make it more tender (lactic acid hinders the formation of gluten) and got a paler, denser waffle, crisp on the outside and very tender inside with a slightly tangy flavor. When he used cake flour with a little cornmeal for crunch, he finally had what he was looking for: a waffle with the texture of a crisp-crusted souffle, with a bit of a cornmeal crunch and a nice buttery tang. It went well with butter and maple syrup, but he also liked it as a base for a vanilla- and spice-scented compote of dried fruits.

It's important to not let waffles sit; they lose their crispness quickly. But they freeze well.

CORNMEAL WAFFLES WITH WINTER FRUIT

Makes 6 Waffles

COMPOTE	WAFFLES
2 CUPS WATER	3/4 CUP CAKE FLOUR
1 CUP SUGAR	1/4 CUP CORNMEAL
1 (3-INCH) SECTION VANILLA BEAN	1 TABLESPOON PLUS 1 TEASPOON SUGAR
2 WHOLE CLOVES	2 TEASPOONS BAKING POWDER
1 CUP DRIED APRICOTS	1/2 TEASPOON BAKING SODA
1 CUP PITTED PRUNES	1/4 TEASPOON SALT
1/2 CUP DRIED SOUR CHERRIES, OPTIONAL	2 EGGS, SEPARATED
	1 CUP BUTTERMILK
	1/2 CUP SOUR CREAM

COMPOTE

Bring water and sugar to boil in medium saucepan. Split vanilla bean lengthwise and, using tip of small sharp knife, scrape seeds into saucepan. Add bean pod and cloves to saucepan and continue cooking 5 minutes.

Reduce heat to low and add apricots, prunes and cherries. Cook at bare simmer just until fruit plumps and softens, 10 to 15 minutes.

Remove vanilla bean before serving. Leftovers can be stored, covered and refrigerated.

WAFFLES

Sift together flour, cornmeal, sugar, baking powder, baking soda and salt in large bowl. Stir together egg yolks, buttermilk and sour cream in medium bowl. Beat egg whites in third bowl until stiff peaks form.

Quickly combine egg yolk-sour cream mixture and dry ingredients, stirring just until batter takes on pebbly texture. Fold in egg whites.

Pour batter in waffle iron and bake according to manufacturer's instruction. Top with Winter Fruit Compote and serve immediately.

Each waffle with 1/4 cup Winter Fruit Compote:
415 calories; 317 mg sodium; 81 mg cholesterol; 7 grams fat; 86 grams carbohydrates; 7 grams protein; 1.28 grams fiber.

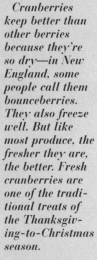

Cranberries keep better than other berries because they're so dry—in New England, some people call them bounceberries. They also freeze well. But like most produce, the fresher they are, the better. Fresh cranberries are one of the traditional treats of the Thanksgiving-to-Christmas season.

This simple dish was a holiday specialty of Times Staff Writer Russ Parsons' mother. All it needs is eight minutes' cooking time— and then a three-day wait. When the Test Kitchen first made it, the dish disappeared within minutes. We think it is one of the very best ways to use fresh cranberries.

MOM PARSONS' CRANBERRIES

Makes 2 1/2 Cups

1 1/2 CUPS SUGAR

3/4 CUP WATER

3 WHOLE CLOVES

3 WHOLE ALLSPICE

2 (3-INCH) CINNAMON STICKS

1 (12-OUNCE) BAG FRESH CRANBERRIES

GRATED ZEST OF 1 ORANGE

Bring sugar, water, cloves, allspice and cinnamon sticks to boil in 4-quart saucepan. Cook, stirring, until syrup is clear, about 3 minutes. Add cranberries and cook just until they begin to pop, about 5 minutes.

Remove from heat, add grated orange zest and cool. Refrigerate at least 3 days before using.

Each 1/4-cup serving:
132 calories; 1 mg sodium; 0 cholesterol; 0 fat; 35 grams carbohydrates; 0 protein; 0.41 gram fiber.

Photography Credits

Mark Boster, page 107

Bob Carey, pages 41, 101, 108, 119

Robert Durell, page 124

Patrick Downs, pages 22, 57, 61, 129

Gary Friedman, pages 37, 120, 123, 137

Robert Gauthier, pages 31, 59, 63, 89

Lawrence K. Ho, pages 20, 27, 47, 53

Randy Leffingwell, pages 115, 131

Kirk McKoy, pages 28, 77, 84, 127, 133

Rick Meyer, pages 64, 73, 81, 87

Paul Morse, cover, back cover,
pages 19, 25, 39, 55, 69, 93, 95, 97, 103, 135

Anacleto Rapping, pages 17, 51

Perry C. Riddle, pages 79, 122

Iris Schneider, pages 71, 78

Al Seib, pages 75, 83, 113

Food styling by Donna Deane, Mayi Brady and Julianne Tantum

Photo production by Times Photo Imaging Specialist Rikki Sax

Acknowledgments

Numerous people contributed to the production of this book.
In particular, the Food Editor would like to thank the following:

Davilynn Furlow, for keeping everything organized and everyone calm;
Tracy Crowe McGonigle, for a beautiful package, for getting the most out
of two colors and for accomplishing the impossible feat of juggling her
duties for the Food section and the book project;
Charles "Rewrite King" Perry, for many well-written headnotes;
Russ Parsons, for his bountiful In the Kitchen recipes;
Barbara Hansen, for her recipe wisdom;
Donna Deane, for running the greatest Test Kitchen, a refuge for us all;
Nick Cuccia, for keeping the section going when everyone else was dis-
tracted with the book project; Cindy Dorn, for keeping the outside world at
bay and for organizing the office renovation when everyone was too busy
to help; Kathy Gosnell, for her sharp copy editing when the recipes
were originally published in the paper;
and Anne Colby, for her objective look at the book proofs.

Don Michel for keeping the book project on track and handling
the details of printing and shipping; Narda Zacchino,
for encouraging us to make the book a priority;
Tom Trapnell, for sharing Tracy Crowe McGonigle on this project;
and Shelby Coffey, for always setting high standards.

Los Angeles Times photographers Mark Boster, Bob Carey, Robert Durell,
Patrick Downs, Gary Friedman, Robert Gauthier, Lawrence K. Ho,
Con Keyes, Randy Leffingwell, Kirk McKoy, Rick Meyer, Paul Morse,
Anacleto Rapping, Perry C. Riddle, Iris Schneider and Al Seib for their
always excellent pictures in this book and in the weekly section;
and Rikki Sax, for scanning the photos.

Regular contributors Marion Cunningham, Rose Dosti, Joan Drake,
Michelle Huneven and Abby Mandel, for their well-loved columns and
stories. And the many writers, chefs and home cooks who contributed
recipes to the section and the book.

Mayi Brady, for testing the tough recipes and our Food section interns, past
and present, Phil Andres, Charity Ferreira, Shoshana Goldberg, Jim Hall,
Jana Lieblich, May Parich, Angela Pettera, Alisa Schwartz
and Julianne Tantum, for inspiring new ideas;
Bruce Henstell, for his essential recipe nutritional analyses.

Finally, Jonathan Gold, Bill Furlow and Tom McGonigle, the spouses who
spent many late evenings and weekends without their partners;
and especially Isabel Ochoa Gold and Colin and Brendan McGonigle,
who went to bed too many nights without their moms.

Index

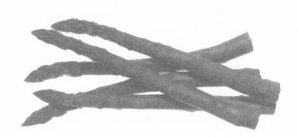